Writing for Religious and Other Specialty Markets

Writing for Religious and Other Specialty Markets

Dennis E. Hensley
Rose A. Adkins

BROADMAN PRESS
Nashville, Tennessee

© Copyright 1987 • Broadman Press
All Rights Reserved

ISBN: 0-8054-4279-11
Dewey Decimal Classification: 808
Subject Heading: AUTHORSHIP//CHURCH
LITERATURE//PERIODICALS
Library of Congress Catalog Number: 87-667
Printed in the United States of America

Library of Congress Cataloging-in-Publication Data

Hensley, Dennis E., 1948-
  Writing for religious and other specialty markets.

  1. Christian literature—Authorship.   2. Authorship.
I. Adkins, Rose.   II. Title.
BR44.H46   1987   808'.02   87-667
ISBN 0-8054-7911-2 (pbk.)

Dedications

To Ron, Jim, Bill, and Tim—four brothers-in-law who have been like real brothers to me.

—Dennis E. Hensley

To my children for their patience with me, to *Writer's Digest* for its many years of teaching me, and to my best friend Gene for always believing in me.

—Rose A. Adkins

Acknowledgments

We wish to thank Bill Brohaugh, editor of *Writer's Digest,* Tom Noton, editor of *The Christian Writer,* and Marilyn Bailey, editor of *The Inkling,* for allowing us to reprint herein sections of our published works which have previously appeared in their periodicals. Special thanks to Sharon Mowrer for meticulous typing and proofreading.

Contents

About the Authors

Dennis E. Hensley holds a Ph.D. in English from Ball State University, where he taught composition from 1974-78. From 1978-82, he was Director of Publications at Manchester College. Since 1982, he has been a full-time freelance writer. He is a Regional Correspondent for *Writer's Digest*, a monthly columnist for *The Christian Writer*, and a contributing editor for *Insight, ShopTalk, The Ball State University Forum,* and *Pace: Piedmont Airline's Inflight Magazine*. A former reporter for *The Muncie Star*, Dr. Hensley has published more than fifteen-hundred freelance articles in *Reader's Digest, The Baptist Bulletin, The Writer, Modern Bride, Contact, Spirit, The War Cry* and *Inkling*, among many others. His twelve books include *Uncommon Sense* and *Positive Workaholism, The Freelancer* and the Christian novel *The Legacy of Lillian Parker* which he wrote under the pen name of Leslie Holden. He and his wife, Rose, live in Fort Wayne, Indiana, with their children, Nathan and Jeanette.

Rose A. Adkins was editor of *Writer's Market* from 1971-75, and associate editor of *Writer's Digest* from 1975-84. Her articles, stories, and poems have been published in *The Cincinnati Enquirer Sunday Magazine, The Christian Writer, Family Circle, Marian Helpers Bulletin, Pro Quarterback, Writer's Yearbook,* and many others. She is coauthor of *The Beginning Writer's Answer Book,* and she wrote the "Help!" column for *Writer's Digest* from 1980-84. She is a frequent participant in writers' conferences, seminars, and workshops, and is currently working as a freelance writer, editor, and consultant in Cincinnati.

Guest Preface:

Special Writers for Specialty Markets

When I initiated "Pen Tips," my marketing column in *The Christian Writer* magazine, marketing was a lot easier. A writer could sit down and produce an article that might fit in any number of general-interest periodicals. If one editor rejected it, the writer simply sent it on to another editor.

Since then, however, many of those same markets have pulled in their sights and have targeted their publications with a much narrower focus. For example, whereas we used to have several general women's magazines, we now have such specialized periodicals as *Today's Secretary, The Homemaker, Ms Magazine, Women in Business,* and *Working Mother*—to name just a few.

Scanning the rows of periodicals on the neighborhood newsstand or reviewing the latest magazine listings is a marketing exercise that boggles the mind. One cannot help but wonder how there can be enough interested consumers to support such highly specialized publications as *Today's OR Nurse, The Dispensing Optician,* or *American Ink Makers.* But, obviously, there are readers who desire what these periodicals have to offer.

This ongoing trend toward specialization has moved the freelance writer into an entirely new career realm. Most articles must now be slanted toward a narrower, more specialized audience—rarely to "people" in the overarching, general sense.

What this all means is that you, the freelancer, must be able to understand the unique needs of these targeted groups; you must know how to properly query their editors; and you must be able to present your articles in formats that are so appropriate there will be no doubt that they actually will be purchased. Otherwise, the chances of selling your manuscripts to other somewhat similar publications (should you even be able to find some) will be slim.

A beginning writer once wrote to me with the complaint that an article he had written to fit an unusual word length and to serve a special audience had been rejected. He was venting his frustration because he now would not be able to sell the material elsewhere without rewriting it extensively. Part of his problem—and the probable reason for his article's rejection—was his lack of knowledge concerning the market he was trying to break into. He needed advice on how to slant his article appropriately for specialized audiences and how to include in it the proper quotes, statistics, research, announcements, case histories, and speculations which would captivate an editor's interest.

That is why this book was written: to help you learn how to write for and sell to the specialty markets.

As writers, it's part of our ongoing responsibility to learn all we can about the markets for which we write. Personally, I am delighted to see a book that will increase my knowledge and understanding of the specialized markets and of the readers who will ultimately benefit from my writing endeavors.

Such a book fulfills a twofold need. It helps all of us, as writers, to write more knowledgeably for a particular field; it also increases the chances that each of these specialized markets will receive the kinds of submissions that will more closely meet their editorial needs.

I've worked with Dr. Dennis E. Hensley since 1980, both at writers' conferences and on the staff of *The Christian Writer* magazine. I don't know anyone who has a greater understanding or more varied experience with specialty magazines. By his own example, he has taught me that any writer with the proper background knowledge and attendant flexibility can write for almost any periodical. He has been a constant reminder to me and other freelancers that we must seek new levels of interest and understanding, and that we must specialize, specialize, specialize.

Rose Adkins was the perfect choice as Dr. Hensley's coauthor on this project. I have admired her career and writing know-how, through *Writer's Digest,* since I started my own writing career in 1969. Her involvement with the *Writer's Market* book for seven years more than qualifies her as an expert on the current multitude of specialty markets.

Together they have produced a book that will change the way writers write—and help make each of us a writing specialist.

—Sally E. Stuart
Contributing Editor
The Christian Writer

Introduction:

The Age of Specialty Markets

During the many years I was associate editor of *Writer's Digest,* I was responsible for proofreading the editorial content of each month's issue. I didn't mind. How else would I have had time to read the trade magazine, what with my busy schedule of working full time, caring for my family of eight children, and pursuing my own efforts at freelance writing and marketing? Spare time—especially spare time for reading—was practically nonexistent. Reading the trade journals which would help me to learn more about writing and selling was something I rarely found time for. In fact, reading of any kind usually was scheduled in last place on my "to-do" lists.

But help was on the way.

When I was editing the *Writer's Market* annual editions in the early 1970s, the age of specialization was just beginning. Along with the birth of new publications, which were listed in each annual edition, came the demise of many others. (We tactfully used the term "folding" when we spoke of magazines that were dying or failing in the marketplace.)

During that period, publishers were trying desperately to present editorial content that would appeal to mass audiences. Every year there were literally hundreds of new publications made available to the reading public, but most failed to become successful. They folded after three or four issues due to a lack of reader interest (which was quickly followed by a loss of advertising revenue and financial backing). Publishers of new magazines who directed their editorial content toward a mass general readership almost always found themselves headed for failure.

Because I also was writing "The Market Column" for *Writer's Digest* during those years, I was in a position to see the phenomenal moving trend toward specialty markets that was developing. I was in a choice seat and felt privileged during that time because I, too, was writing for specialty magazines, particularly in the religious and inspirational field.

Magazines which were aimed toward a specific readership, with editorial content specialized for that readership, were more likely to be successful. The age of specialization, in those early years, had begun before many writers even knew what specialty markets were. Writers soon discovered, however, that they no longer had to be limited to only a few subjects to write about. Their options were soon expanded tremendously. They had many specialty topics to report on and the increasing number of these markets was becoming surprisingly rewarding for them.

Things haven't changed much in the freelance marketplace since that time, except to get even better. One reason writers have even more specialty markets to write for, and more subjects in which to specialize, is because readers today are busier than ever. Most often their daily jobs occupy more than eight hours, and much of their reading is now replaced by the six-o'clock news on television.

It's now hard to imagine that at one time people actually

read the entire newspaper every day and subscribed to many general-interest magazines to satisfy their curious minds and various reading interests and needs. But today, people are turning to specialty magazines for knowledge, trends, and current information about their chosen careers and special interests.

From a professional standpoint, understanding this market isn't as simple as merely saying that specialty magazines are geared to the special interests of readers. Indeed, something this far-reaching—which brings a multitude of opportunities such as we now have in specialty markets—has nothing "simple" about it at all.

Consider, for example, how varied the specialty markets are: there's everything from *Antiques Monthly* for collectors to *Audio Magazine* for high-fidelity buffs to *Barrister* for young lawyers. The number of specialty magazines is growing and with that growth comes a continuous need for good material from freelance writers.

We can assume that because the number of general interest magazines has declined and the growth of special interest magazines has been quite dramatic, consumers prefer to buy a magazine that promises that all its pages will be of interest to them. "Consumer publications" concentrate on pastime interests of readers, whereas "trade journals" concentrate on their occupations.

To more clearly define what specialty magazines are, let's look at magazines for women, of which there currently are more than seventy such active and successful publications, ranging from *Virtue* to *Family Circle* to *Ladies' Home Journal*. Sometimes their titles alone will indicate their specific readership and required editorial slant, as in *Working Woman* and *Farm Woman News* and *Today's Christian Woman* and *Modern Bride*. *Self* is on the women's magazines list, and its editorial content is directed solely toward individual self-improvement, whereas another women's magazine, *Family Circle,* is almost entirely family oriented.

When writing for general magazines, it's much more difficult to hone editorial interests. General, after all, means "general," whereas specialty markets indicate something very finely tuned to specific interests and editorial content.

Editors know what kind of people are reading their specialty magazines, and they also know what those people expect to be offered editorially. Because of this, freelance writing assignments are more definite. Articles are more precisely planned and directed, which is extremely helpful to writers.

Specialty markets range from quarterly academic journals to monthly popular magazines. Most trade journals serve a specific industry, but some industries have competing trade publications. Trade journals always need anecdotes about businesses. They also use many short business profiles. Company publications are also good specialty markets. Many companies cannot afford a full-time staff to provide editorial content, so they rely on freelance writers. In short, opportunities are abounding.

Specialty markets for writers of religious and inspirational material are even more far-reaching and plentiful. There are newsletters and small magazines geared specifically to the needs and interests of inspirational writers, and they make available a continuing network of news and opportunity. Most denominations have at least one publication for clergy and one for laity, and almost all of these publications use freelance material.

Among the more general, interdenominational magazines are *Moody Monthly* with more than three-hundred thousand copies in circulation, *Christian Herald* with a two-hundred thousand circulation, and certain journals which are directed toward ministers, such as *Christianity Today* with an almost two-hundred thousand circulation and *The Christian Century* with about thirty-five thousand.

A major focus of this book will be to show you how to write for these magazines. You will learn how to study them carefully and understand their editorial position and their reader interests.

Subjects for specialty religion publications, as well as for religious and inspirational books, include spiritual renewal, marriage and family counseling, personal experiences, self-help ideas for Christian living, church growth, prayer and devotions, Bible studies, and conversion stories.

By reading the religion section of your weekend newspapers, you can spot news of current trends that may suggest a book theme or perhaps a report or interview that can be further developed into a feature article.

Secular newspapers often will buy freelance articles about churches in their publication area. Writing a few church-related news stories for your local paper can help improve your writing status, increase your income, and help you to gain expertise.

There are more than seventeen-hundred religion-oriented magazines today. Religious publications include denominational magazines and journals; Sunday school take-home papers; general magazines; magazines for women, men, children, young people, and families. There are also theological journals, trade publications, regional church publications, house organs of various religious organizations, and religious educational materials. Other freelance opportunities for writers include church newsletters, religious radio and television programming, and motion pictures. Cable television is actively producing religious programming and there has been a steady increase in religious radio broadcasting. Publishers are also buying poetry for Christian and inspirational greeting cards.

The Christian Booksellers Association estimates that five thousand new Christian-oriented books are published annually. Sales of religious books and publications exceed $600 million each year. These statistics prove there is a phenomenal amount of freelance work available for eager and talented writers.

Inspirational writing is an excellent area of writing for beginners, and is, in fact, how I broke into freelancing many years ago, long before I had even heard of *Writer's Digest* or knew what a trade journal or specialty market was. The pay may not have been as good as other writing specialties, but the vast marketing possibilities and diversity of subjects were certainly promising for a beginner.

Specialization—achieving expert status in a specialty area such as health, the environment, self-improvement, or inspiration/religion—is one of the surest ways of getting into print these days. You can, of course, choose to be a generalist writer, and some freelancers find it profitable to do this; but for quick and early success, I always tell freelancers to begin with specialization.

The ability to write well on a variety of topics is certainly the mark of a talented writer, but earning sure money and gaining expert status in at least one or two specialty areas is often more practical for a freelancer. This usually leads to a full career anyway. For example, most specialty writers eventually write a book about one of their chosen topics. Publishers are eager to assign book contracts to writers who have many magazine credits on one topic—writers who can promise to turn out a solid how-to book on their subject of expertise.

But first the expertise has to be discovered, developed, published, and publicized. And that's why training books like this one are needed.

Most writers "broke into" freelancing by writing about things they already were experts in. For example, my coauthor, Dennis E. Hensley, worked as a music teacher and disc jockey part time during his high school and college years. Appropriately, his first freelance articles were about music topics and his earliest bylines appeared in *Music Journal, Downbeat, Guitar Player, Stereo,* and *Music City News.* Having established himself as a freelance writer, he then began to write for a variety of non-music-related periodicals. You, too, can break into freelancing by writing about your area of knowledge, whether it be woodworking, sewing, or running computers.

A writer has a good chance of selling a how-to article on working with the handicapped if he has worked as a volunteer with a health agency, has had personal experience working with a handicapped person, or is himself handicapped in some way. An article on how to restore an automobile has a better chance of selling to a specialty magazine if the writer has restored her own car or witnessed step-by-step the restoration of a neighbor's or friend's.

But does this mean you *have* to be an expert on a topic in order to write about it? Certainly not. A writer once told me,

"If an editor needs an article on a subject I know absolutely nothing about, I never let that editor know about my ignorance. That's what *research* is all about."

That writer went on to explain that the library was filled with magazines and books on almost every topic, and that researching (learning new information) was what made writing challenging and exciting. Writers grow and improve by conducting research.

Besides, there are living experts on virtually every subject. Interviews can be done with these experts which will make articles more authoritative and interesting. A wealth of knowledge is available if writers are willing to accept a challenge. Through such research and interviewing of experts on any given topic, many freelancers have built their credit lists and developed expertise in areas they knew little about at the start.

During the years I wrote the "Help!" column for *Writer's Digest,* one question was frequently asked of me by writers: "Do the specialty magazines and trade journals pay as poorly as they used to?" Throughout the industry, editors are willing to pay good rates for quality work derived from thorough research and crisp writing directed to the special interests of the readers. As competition continues to increase within the specialty markets, editors will continue to strive for top writing to present to their readers. Rates have increased as the quality of writing has improved over the years. This trend will continue.

Reasons why you might want to write for the specialty markets are obvious: they are there, they need good material from freelance writers, and you can easily and adequately develop an expertise for writing for any number of them.

Do you need any more reasons than those to write for today's specialty markets? I think not. So, come along now and explore the rest of this fact-filled book and learn how you, too, can become a successful freelance writer in the specialty markets.

—Rose A. Adkins

1

Becoming Motivated to Write

Robert Louis Stevenson once said, "I hate to write, but I love to have written." Building up the motivation to face that piece of blank paper is a challenge. That is why, before we begin to look at writing or marketing techniques, we first are going to try to get you motivated to become a writer.

Four Motivational Words

Frequently, I am asked to serve as a keynote speaker at writers' conferences around the country. One of my favorite speech topics focuses upon four motivational words for writers.

The first word is attitude.

Writers need to have confident attitudes about their work. They can, too, if they will remember to repeat this expression during times of despair: "I am unique, and that is what gives my writing sales potential."

Have you ever considered how truly unique you are? For a fact, you are the only person God created exactly that way. There never before has been a human being exactly like you, and there never will be again. No one else will have your exact features, behavior patterns, expressions, and feelings. You are the only one who will have your particular perspective.

What's more, I will not live your life—*you* will! As such, I will not be everywhere—you will be, I will not read everything you will read, I will not face the same problems you will face, nor experience the same laughter or tears which these problems will ultimately lead to.

You are the only person with your exact perspective on life. And this gives you unique creativity. You know why? Because you can do something no one else can: you can explain things *your* way. It will be this fresh, individualistic, one-of-a-kind approach that will make your writings marketable. So, don't stifle your individualism.

Your attitude must be one of confidence, something that insists you have the uniqueness to give your writing real sales potential.

The second word is perspective.

As a beginning writer, you need to have a long-range perspective of things. Too often, writers receive two or three rejection slips and they give up on freelancing. With long-range perspective, it can be seen that rejection slips prove you've mounted the first rung of your ladder to success as a writer.

One must realize early in a writing career (as with any other career) that trial and error are part of the development process. Charles Kettering, the engineering genius at General Motors, once noted, "We have come to fear failure too much. Failure is the *practice* essential to success."

No one is perfect at anything during the early stages. A baseball pitcher throws many a wild pitch before he makes it to the major leagues. A concert pianist hits many a sour note before she performs in Carnegie Hall. A Nobel prize winner in literature receives many a rejection slip before earning the ultimate honors.

The good news about rejection slips is that they are first-round encounters and not end results in themselves. Get the proper perspective: you are not a failure, you are a novice. Your day will come. Hang in there.

Don't expect too much from yourself too soon. Just because you know the alphabet, can spell and type, that doesn't mean you can become a professional writer in four months. Would it be logical for me to say that since I have a driver's license, I should be able to compete in the Indianapolis 500 if I get a few weeks of race-driving practice?

Keep your perspective. Love your work as a writer. Be excited about it. Maintain your enthusiasm for your career. Don't let rejection slips bother you. There are many reasons why articles don't get accepted, even when they are good. Maybe the magazine was overstocked on material. Maybe the magazine already had a similar article or story on file. Maybe the editor was depressed that day over personal problems and rejected everything. Perhaps the editor was worried that something in your article might offend a major advertiser. Keep your perspective. A rejection slip only means that a particular editor did not want to buy a particular manuscript on a particular day.

Continue to try. Nobody ever sold a manuscript by leaving it in a drawer. Don't take it personally. *You* weren't rejected. Your *manuscript* was. Try the same magazine with something new. Keep a lot of manuscripts in the mail. That way, when a rejection comes, it'll just be one-tenth of your total circulating material. Never lose your perspective on things: minor setbacks are just part of the developing process.

The third word is discipline.

It is great to attend writers' conferences. It's wonderful to read writing trade magazines. It's fantastic to study self-help books on freelance writing. It's smart to be involved in a local writers' club. But the knowledge you gain from each of these learning experiences is *useless* until you apply it.

All your life you've heard the expression "knowledge is power." That's only half true. Knowledge alone is not powerful. Actually, it is *applied* knowledge that is power.

You can't just think about writing, you've got to *do* the writing. You can't simply develop the idea for a book, you've got to write the book. You can't stare at the typewriter keys, you've got to pound them. In short, you can't merely *hope* to be a writer, you've got to start *being* a writer.

Maintain your discipline. Paderewski, the great pianist, once told an interviewer, "If I miss practicing one day, I know it. If I miss practicing one week, the critics know it. If I miss practicing one month, the public knows it."

If we don't have the discipline needed to be productive as writers, we cannot expect to get rewards. A boss once sent a memo to one of his workers: "Dear Employee, I've given you a raise in salary. It will become effective when you do."

Are you disciplined enough to give yourself a raise?

The fourth word is vision.

The Bible says, "Where there is no vision, the people perish" (Prov. 29:18). That also applies to writers who do not have goals. You can't hit a bull's-eye unless you have a target. You must conceive a vision of where you want your career to be in one year, one decade, one lifetime.

There are good reasons for continually setting higher goals for yourself. The process makes you strive harder and it shows you that you have more ability than you personally realized.

Have you ever seen a flea circus? Little fleas can be trained to do things similar to large circus animals and, when reduced to small sizes, provide the viewer with many laughs.

However, there's something interesting about how these fleas are trained.

If you place a few fleas inside a jar and screw a lid on top, the fleas will instantly try to escape. They will jump up a dozen times or so and hit themselves against the lid. In a moment, however, they are able to gauge the lid's range. In all subsequent jumps they will leap *almost* to the lid, but not actually ram themselves against it.

Thereafter, an amazing thing can be done.

The lid from the jar can be removed completely, yet the fleas will continue to jump only as high as the lid *used* to be. They are convinced, after having hit themselves against the former lid, that they are limited in the height they may ever reach.

This is analogous to people who have experienced a few failures in life and, thereafter, have decided they are incapable of even reaching the success heights they once attained to. Like the fleas, they reduced their goals to low "safe" levels; but, also like the fleas, they remain trapped and bottled.

It is better for writers to be like a mechanical mouse: when the mouse bumps into an obstacle, it turns and immediately heads in a new direction. Eventually, it reaches its ultimate goal. You can, too, if you keep your vision on your target.

There you have it: four words to live by—*attitude, perspective, discipline,* and *vision.* Remember them. Use them.

As you apply these words to your life and become motivated about a career in writing, you will want to channel that motivation in the right directions. One direction should head you toward a formal writing class where you will get specific help in developing your writing style.

Perhaps you have already considered the idea of registering for a writing class, but you just haven't known where to look or what to study. Let's take a moment to review some specifics about finding and registering for a writing class.

Selecting a Writing Class

From the time I was a senior in high school, I knew I wanted to be a professional writer. When I enrolled in college I registered for virtually every variety of writing class that was offered. Now, in retrospect, I can honestly say that those classes taught me everything I needed to know about writing *except* how to earn a living as an author. Unfortunately, that was the one thing I was hoping they *would* teach me.

In my "composition" classes I learned how to write a theme and a term paper. To date, I've never sold a term paper or a theme to any magazines. In "creative writing" classes I was asked to try my hand at stream-of-conscious short-story writing and experimental poetry. It all helped me think in new ways, but it has never put a nickel in my pocket nor added a by-line credit to my resumé.

Here was the dilemma: *writing classes should be taught by working writers, but few seldom are.* That was true when I was eighteen, and it's still true today.

If you want to become a surgeon, you don't study under someone who has read about surgery in books but never has been in an operating room. Nevertheless, that is what far too often goes on in writing classes: people who've never published a book nor written an article wind up lecturing to students on how to be writers. It's illogical. ("Said Simple Simon to the pieman, *'Let me taste your wares.'*")

Each year I teach thirty one-day freelance writing workshops around the country. These six-hour crash courses provide a complete overview of basic writing techniques, marketing procedures, and copyright laws. For someone wanting an indoctrination into freelance writing, these workshops are the very thing.

But where do you go after the workshop?

After you've reviewed your workshop notes, studied the handouts, and read the book on writing you probably purchased that day, you are ready to make some serious attempts at writing. You need to find a writing class where you can be encouraged, critiqued, taught, and challenged. How do you go about it?

First of all, try to discover just how many writing classes are being taught in your area. Make calls to the public library, the local arts council, the YMCA/YWCA, the area writers' clubs, and the continuing-education offices of your city and state colleges. Try to find a class that meets at least once per week for ten to fifteen weeks.

Inquire about the age group of the enrollees. If you are a senior citizen, you may not wish to be amidst a group of high schoolers; conversely, if you are a young person, you may wish to seek a mixed-age group so that you can benefit from other people's experiences.

The class should be made up of twenty or fewer students if it is primarily a lecture course or thirty students if it is a combination of part lecture and part small critique group exchanges. Never take more than one writing class per semester; reach subject mastery before you attempt diversity.

If possible, get permission to sit in on one class session during a semester prior to the semester you intend to enroll in. This will give you first-hand knowledge of how the class is run. Talk to the present students and ask if they feel they are learning much.

The cost of the class should be of concern to you only to the degree that it properly reflects the value of the course. For example, it's very possible to enroll in a local writers' club ten-week private class for as low as twenty-five dollars per person. However, if these are mere "chat sessions," you'll be wasting your time and money. Conversely, a fifteen-week continuing-education night-school class might cost you as much as three-hundred dollars. Yet, if it's taught by an author who can train you to write a book proposal that will earn you a twenty-five-hundred-dollar advance, it will be money well invested. (And don't forget that registration fees, books, and transportation to and from class are all tax-deductible items.)

Your writing course instructor should be a working writer who has had experience in dealing and working with editors and publishers and perhaps even literary agents. To discover whether the teacher has published anything recently, look up his or her name in *Books in Print* and in the *Reader's Guide to Periodical Literature* at your library.

Your teacher should be someone who offers useful, pragmatic lectures regarding what does and doesn't sell in the marketplace. He or she should be a meticulous grader of your written submissions; someone who shows you where you had grammatical, punctuation, spelling, and stylistic errors. The teacher should criticize and evaluate your writing, but also laud you for your progress. The evaluation procedure should also include feedback from other members of the class.

It will be of long-range value to you if your teacher is the kind who gives handout materials which you can keep on file for postclass reference. As a teacher, myself, I've given my students sample book contracts, sample query letters, suggested reading lists, copies of my published articles, lists of interview questions, and tip sheets on how to use a camera.

All effective teachers prepare a syllabus in advance of class. Ask to see a copy of it. Pay particular attention to the lecture topics your teacher plans to cover. Will they be of use to the kind of writing career you hope to develop?

Also check to see if any field trips are planned (to a newspaper or magazine office), if there will be any guest speakers in class (editors, literary agents, publishers), what sort of online experience you will gain (two assignments for the campus newspaper, an interview for the writing club's anthology issue), and what your texts for the class will be.

The more confidence you have in your teacher, the more energetic you will be about attending class sessions and taking part in class activities and assignments.

Naturally, no matter how competent any teacher is, it ultimately is the student who determines how much he or she will benefit from the class. In short, the responsibility for learning is your own.

Don't enroll in the class with the expectation that you will be a top-notch professional writer fifteen weeks later. Be realistic in your expectations and use your class time wisely. Attend sessions faithfully and maximize the time.

Keep current on all your reading and writing assignments. As you encounter new challenges, note your questions and bring them up in class. Write something each day so that you can put your new knowledge into immediate use.

Maintain a courteous respect for your teacher. Do not bring a dozen of your manuscripts to class and ask the instructor to read and evaluate them for you. Let the teacher be in charge of how the learning process will proceed.

P. G. Wodehouse once noted, "Success comes to a writer, as a rule, so gradually that it is always something of a shock to him to look back and realize the heights to which he has climbed." I agree with this. Climbing those heights can be made easier, however, with the help of a good writing teacher. Find one.

In the discipline of studying under a good teacher, never forget that much of the learning process will call for a degree of personal professional development on your own. Let's now see ways in which you can enhance this procedure.

Points of Professionalism

I was invited once to serve on a panel at the national convention of Women in Communication. One young lady in the audience asked the panel to list some procedures and habits which professional authors follow. The host asked me to field the question. Here are some of the points of professionalism I advised that audience:

First, *carry two books with you everywhere you go*. One book will be filled with blank pages so that you can jot down any good ideas whenever they hit you. If you hear an interesting statistic, a new vocabulary word, or an unusual name, write it down immediately. If you suddenly think of a good short story idea, clever book title, or new article concept, write it down right then. Never trust your memory.

The other book you'll carry (in a purse or sportcoat pocket) will be something to read. Writers must constantly be expanding their reserves of knowledge, and the best way to do that is by constant reading. By carrying a book with you, you can read two chapters while waiting in the dentist's office or six pages as a train passes before your car or a few paragraphs while you wait for the elevator. You'll be amazed at how much extra reading you'll be able to do each year by always carrying a lightweight paperback book to read.

Second, *have business cards printed with your name, your profession ("Freelance Writer"), your address, and your phone number on them*. Most people don't really know what a freelance writer is or what he or she does. They will ask you, "But what newspaper or magazine do you *work* for?" Just respond that you are an independent writer based in your local city and that you do assignments for a variety of publications. Your business card will add a sense of permanence to what may be conceived of by many people as a gadfly career. If you have a phone and a mailing address, most people will accept you as a legitimate worker (and that's extremely important when you are trying to get a secretary to let you see her boss or you need to get a loan from a cautious banker).

Another great benefit of business cards is that by handing them out you begin to build your network of sources. If a newsworthy event happens in a local neighborhood, at a church, or at a small business, and people have your business cards handy, who do you think they are going to call to give their news to? This provides you with a constant source of story leads.

Third, *maintain your folders and files of all previous research*. If you write an involved article for your local newspaper about the history of the old courthouse on the square, that's *your* story. If that courthouse should ever burn down, editors will turn to you to write a feature about it. If you've thrown out your notes and photo negatives, you'll have to forfeit the assignment.

Professional writers do not discard research; they use it as a springboard for new assignments. This year, for example, you might write a feature for your local paper on the Smithville, Indiana, Courthouse. Next year you can combine that research with new research on the Jonesville, Ohio,

Courthouse and sell this expanded feature to a travel magazine as, "Old Courthouses of the Midwest." You've doubled your money, yet cut your research and writing time in half.

Fourth, *remember the five letter Ps: be prompt, persistent, professional, polished, and paid.* A prompt writer shows up early or on time for interview appointments and never misses his submission deadlines. A persistent reporter stays on the job; he digs, questions, and researches until the full story has been uncovered. A professional writer is a competent worker who writes well, interviews well, protects sources, thinks creatively, and assists his editors. A polished writer respects his profession and, as such, dresses smartly and behaves mannerly so that he will always reflect well on the writing profession. A hardworking writer merits good payment for his writings and is not hesitant to quote a fee worthy of his professional services.

Fifth, *write something a minimum of five days per week.* Writing is a discipline which must be enhanced through regular practice. The part-time writer who puts in a fifteen-hour marathon writing stint every Saturday will never mature his skills. Powerful writing is developed through daily revision of the previous day's output and nightly subconscious analysis of the ongoing plots, sketches, or articles. Writers are artistic thinkers and creative expressionists; such abilities are not bestowed on those who approach writing in spurts and bursts. That's the difference between a pro and an amateur.

Another important difference between the pro and the amateur is that the professional writer is always excited about a chance to discover a new story. He or she makes constant notes and keeps active "tickler" files about ideas for features. Let's look now at how you can follow that same sort of procedure in generating your own writing ideas.

Building Idea Files

Have you ever awakened in the middle of the night with a great idea for redecorating your house, but by morning you had completely forgotten your idea? Have you ever heard a funny line, joke, or expression and thought you should keep it in mind, but by a week later you'd forgotten it?

Of course you have. We all have experienced that forgetfulness syndrome. The human mind has a limited amount of memory strength. You cannot remember everything you hear; and even if you could, you could not automatically know where to apply the things you've retained to something current.

But writers need anecdotes, facts, sketches, ideas, profiles, and tidbits to keep their writing flow from slowing down. As such, it is important for writers to learn how to preserve useful items. Here are some rules and suggestions.

(1) Never trust your memory. Jack London used to say that scrap paper was cheaper than gray brain matter, and that writers should make notes of anything that strikes them as unusual or interesting. Robert Louis Stevenson always carried two books with him wherever he went: one was something to read and the other was a notebook to record his ideas in.

(2) Keep pads and pencils close to areas where you relax and have time to think: your nightstand near your bed; the glove compartment of your car; and your home library or family room.

(3) Keep a recipe file with cards, dividers, and labels. Instead of recipes, record your ideas. Your categories might be things like "Expressions," "Statistics," "Love," "Hate," "Adults," "Kids," "Church," "Retirement," "Crime," "Hobbies," and "Business." Put them in alphabetical order

and be sure to note the source of any information you record.

(4) You might find it useful to maintain loose-leaf notebooks in which to place character sketches. What you do is this: whenever you are at a party, restaurant, or store and you see an interesting person, take out a piece of paper and write down a full description (height, weight, coloring, mode of dress, tone of voice). Later, you can type your notes on paper and add the character sketch to your notebook. This is not only good practice for you as a budding journalist, but it also stockpiles a lot of characters for when you begin to write fiction.

(5) Keeping "location" sketch notebooks is also helpful. When you visit a park or small town or a modern hospital, you can write a description of it for writing practice and future reference.

W. Somerset Maugham was once asked how he was able to write so many books, plays, and short stories when he only wrote from 9 AM until noon. Replied Maugham, "I write twenty-four hours per day. I only *type* from 9 AM until noon."

Like Maugham, you must be awake to ideas all the time. Take notes, record ideas, save thoughts. Then when you sit down to type, you, too, will be able to be prolific.

Summary

In this opening section we discovered that a freelance writer must develop self-confidence in order to become competitive in the publishing arena. This can be enhanced through guidance from a good writing instructor, but must also be supported by the author's own personal professional development.

In our next section we are going to review some basic aspects of writing and marketing techniques which particularly apply to freelance writing for specialized markets. This first section should have given you the motivation and inspiration you need to continue your reading and studying. So, let's forge ahead.

—Dennis E. Hensley

2

How to Guarantee Manuscript Sales

Seasoned professional writers have learned the basic tricks of the writing trade, and they use these procedures to repeat their writing and marketing success over and over, year after year. Fortunately, these important lessons can be learned by you without the delay and pain of the trial-and-error method. In this section we will endeavor to share with you insights on writing and marketing that will help you think, write, and *sell* like a professional. Let's begin by looking at how to develop a writing style that is short on words but long on message.

Economical Writing

One time a frustrated young freelance writer read that George Bernard Shaw was being paid a dollar per word for his writings. The frustrated young man sent Shaw a dollar and attached a note saying, "Here's a dollar. Send me a word!" Two days later the man received a card from Shaw. On it was written just one word: "Thanks."

Shaw knew that economical writing was effective. It's a lesson we all should heed. Most of the time our writing styles are cumbersome, our facts are tiring, and our quotes are loose and rambling.

Consider vocabulary, for example. Did you know that 25

percent of everything written is composed of these ten words: *a, it, to, in, is, of, the, and, you, that?* That's simple enough, right? So why, then, do we clutter our sentences with bulky, chunky, fat words?

During the Battle of the Bulge, German troops surrounded a unit of the American 101st Airborne Division. The Nazis sent a message to the American commander to have his men drop their weapons and surrender. The commander sent a succinct reply: "Nuts." The Airborne unit held its position until Patton's reinforcements arrived a few days later. Obviously, everybody got the message.

Here then are some basic rules for simplifying our writing:

(1) *If you wouldn't talk that way, don't write that way.* Why write something like, "His compensation and renumeration were balanced in accordance to his current value to his employer" when what you would say in conversation would be, "He was paid what he was worth." Keep things on a basic level.

(2) *Don't hem and haw.* Phrases like "from the data it seems apparent" and "it appears somewhat to be" should be reduced to "it is." Either you know what you are writing about or you don't.

(3) *Think before you write.* Get your facts in sequence; state your most important information early in the article. Don't waste words "building up" to the message of your article. Eliminate needless words, sentences, and paragraphs. In short, think through what you need to say and then write just that.

(4) *Eliminate jargon and terminology.* Instead of writing "the alternating current connection prong," just say "the wall plug." Instead of "the document of mutual and concurrent agreement of record," say "the contract." Don't snow readers

with legalese, academese, or specialty mumbo jumbo. Just communicate.

(5) *Paraphrase long quotes.* If one of your expert sources took two-hundred words to explain what you can summarize in twenty words, use your version and simply credit your source.

(6) *Repackage your material.* By using numbers, as I am in this article, you can eliminate needless transition sentences. Another idea is to use a sidebar (boxed information) to pull a chunk of addenda from your article, yet still offer it as part of your article package.

(7) *Cross out repetitive adverbs and adjectives.* If your verbs and nouns are powerful, they won't need excess support from helper words.

(8) *Take a break between rewrites.* After your first draft is finished, wait an hour or a day or even a week if possible before you edit it and then rewrite it. The colder the manuscript is, the colder your editorial eye will be. And that's good.

(9) *Don't delay the subject in sentences.* The words "there are" and "it is" stall most sentences. They should be avoided. Instead of writing, "It is the nature of baboons to be funny," you should write, "Baboons are naturally funny." Instead of, "There are many sailors who get seasick," write, "Many sailors get seasick."

(10) *Use a possessive apostrophe instead of "of the."* Note how, "The rules of the organization are published" is two words longer than "The organization's rules are published." That can amount to an extra thirty-five needless words in an average one-thousand word article. Condense whenever you can.

Keep your writing as simple as possible. As Solomon once

noted, "A word fitly spoken is like apples of gold in pictures of silver" (Prov. 25:11).

Forecasting Reader Reactions

Tight, economical writing will greatly enhance your ability to communicate with your readers. It will be important for you to review the ten rules of economical writing frequently.

Once having mastered the basics of economical writing, you must begin to develop style control. Your writing style must be strong enough to intrigue the reader while also being guided enough to dominate the reader's attention.

As a nonfiction author, your goal is to write so simply no one can misunderstand your message. Naturally, this must be done with style in order to sustain interest, but simplicity of message always remains your prime objective.

To *ensure* that you are communicating effectively, you must anticipate any questions your readers may have and you must provide answers within the context of your article. Simultaneously, you must fashion your article's various parts so that they will elicit predictable responses from the readers. In short, you must be in control of the reader's thoughts.

Everything about your article must flow so naturally and appear so logical, the reader will never realize he is being led along a predestined line of thought. Everything should blend: the title should be appropriate for what is actually covered in the article; the introduction should set a tone that will be carried throughout the piece; and the facts presented should all be pertinent to the topic being discussed.

People are taught to think and assess things according to patterned responses. The more an author stays within these patterns, the more comfortable the reader will be with the article. The six most common response patterns are as follows:

(1) Present a *problem* and the reader will expect a *solution;*
(2) Summarize the *past* and the reader will expect it to apply somehow to the *present;*
(3) Pose a *question* and the reader will anticipate a forthcoming *answer;*
(4) Explain a *cause* and the reader will want you to explain its *effect;*
(5) Offer a *general* overview of something and the reader will assume you will move eventually to discussing its *specific* aspects; and
(6) Denounce something as *wrong* and the reader will expect you to proclaim what is *right.*

By employing these standard thought processes, you can judge in advance what your reader's reactions will be to your writings. If you present a problem and fail to offer a solution, you will deceive, confuse, and anger your reader. A pleased reader will continue to read the rest of the article.

Every time you introduce a new subject in your article, you must justify its inclusion. The reader must never be left wondering, "What does this have to do with the topic?" By relying on the six-patterned responses, you will always stay on target because you will always know just what the reader is expecting to hear about next.

Newer writers should adhere to a standardized approach to article writing which allows full use of the response patterns. Here are some guides along those lines:

(A) Remember to establish the context of whatever is being

discussed in each section of your article. This can be done by using subtitles, topic sentences, or statements of the problem.

(B) Provide point-blank answers to the *who, what, when, where, why, how,* and *how much* questions which most readers will have about your topic. Provide adequate details and explanations on all matters.

(C) Correlate all of your data and show how your topic specifically relates to the reader as information or entertainment.

(D) End your article with a prediction of how your subject will have an impact upon the future or offer a summary of its present impact.

To hold your reader's interest and to maintain your reins upon his thoughts, you must present no ramblings, tangent ideas, or superfluous thoughts. Article readers don't like surprises; they want straight information presented in an easy-to-follow format. Give it to them and you'll always have a reading audience.

Now, since we said earlier that the article's title should be appropriate for what the article is about, let's look now at how to write a good title.

Article Billboards

When you submit a freelance article to an editor, the first thing he or she reads is its title. That title serves as a billboard for the piece. If it's clever, funny, intriguing, or revealing, it will do much to "sell" your product.

In Jimmy Cagney's movie portrayal of George M. Cohan, there is a scene in which Cohan picks up a copy of *Variety*. The headline reads, "STIX NIX HIX PIX." A boy asks Cohan what the title means. Cohan, amazed at the young man's stupidity, explains, "That's simple. It means small town people aren't attending movies about life in the country."

That scene provides a great lesson for freelance writers. In composing a title for an article, one must always keep in mind who will be reading it. For Cohan (a *Variety* subscriber), the STIX title seemed clever. For the boy, it was gobbledygook.

If you have ever labored over coming up with a good title for an article—one that catches a reader's attention *and* previews what the article will be about—you need no longer worry. There are a dozen standard title formats which you can learn in ten minutes and, thereafter, have a variety of options available for whatever sort of "billboard" your article requires. Let's review them:

> Option One: The Rhyming Title
> Example: It Flies in Skies with Spies
>
> Option Two: The Pun Title
> Example: A Thyme for All Seasonings
>
> Option Three: The Quotation Title
> Example: With Malice Toward None
>
> Option Four: The Alliteration Title
> Example: Tight Turns Taunt Truckers
>
> Option Five: The Contrast Title
> Example: Cold Feelings Over Heated Debate
>
> Option Six: The Unexpected Reversal Title
> Example: One Bad Deed Deserves Another
>
> Option Seven: The Provocative Title
> Example: Minister Officiates at His Parents' Wedding

Option Eight: The Blunt Statement Title
Example: Don't Say It with Flowers

Option Nine: The Challenge Title
Example: Can You Improve Your Health Insurance?

Option Ten: The Terse Summary Title
Example: Hinckley Shoots Reagan

Option Eleven: The Teaching Title
Examples: How to be More Productive
          When To Apply for College
          What Your Home Is Worth

Option Twelve: The Numerical Title
Example: Six Ways to Make Spicy Pumpkin Pie

Since the objective of your title will be to arrest and pique the reader's attention, you may wish to develop several titles based on different options. You then can select the best one.

By the way, don't discard any of the titles that don't survive your first choice. They will come in handy later when you resell your article (multiple market it) to other periodicals. A change in title will make it unique for each market.

I once did an article on my father's work as an ocularist (someone who makes and fits artificial eyes). The first time I sold the article, I used a Pun Title: "The Eyes Have It." The second time I sold it, I used a Quotation Title: "An Eye for an Eye." The third time, I used an Alliteration Title: "Vision Victim Vocation." And so it went, until I had sold the article eight times.

Never just slap a title atop your manuscript. Consider the title to be a sales slogan for your article. Then ask yourself,

"If I were an editor, would *I* be interested in something with this title?"

If your answer is no, keep rewriting it until even *you* are "sold" on it.

Careful Proofreading

If a good title gets your article started right, careful proofreading ends it well. Nothing aggravates an editor more than spelling errors, improperly hyphenated words, typing mistakes, and punctuation flaws. Many times even small, so-called "minor" errors can ruin a manuscript and an author's relationship with an editor or publisher.

I know of one freelance writer whose entire thirty-five-hundred-word article on food preparation techniques was rejected because the author spelled *ptomaine* without the letter p in front. A costly error. (The editor figured that if the writer didn't bother to double check spelling, he might not have bothered to check the other facts in his article. If so, it was too risky to publish it.)

I also know of a writer who accidentally typed "½ cup" instead of "¼" cup in a recipe article. She was responsible for more than a thousand ruined cakes which were prepared by readers of the magazine her article appeared in. The editor received hundreds of complaint letters and dozens of subscription cancellations. Needless to say, that writer no longer has a working relationship with that magazine.

Writers must be careful proofreaders. Fortunately, proofreading isn't difficult to master. The benefits it offers in saved time and money make it worth your attention. Let's quickly review eight tips on how to be more effective at proofreading.

Tip 1: *Read aloud.* Reading something audibly helps you

gauge its rhythm, pace, sound, and degree of difficulty. If you discover that certain passages cause you to be tongue-tied or long-winded, rewrite them in more simplified language.

Tip 2: *Read backward.* Some authors like to dictate rough drafts into a tape recorder. Others like to write everything out in longhand before typing it. Later, when the transcribed copy is read in the same sequence it was dictated or written out, the author often reads into the sentences things that really aren't there.

You may have this problem. Since you already know what your story or article is supposed to say, you may anticipate "ghost" words. To guarantee that you *do* see each word, try reading backward from the last word on a page to the first. In this way, you will notice if a word is misspelled or a period has been forgotten after an abbreviation or a capital letter has been overlooked.

Tip 3: *Use a line screen.* An alternative to reading backward word by word is to use a 5″ x 7″ index card with a razor-cut window ¼ of an inch wide near its top. Simply place the card's window opening over one line of typing at a time. By rapidly moving up the page from the bottom line to the top, you will not be mentally caught up in any sequence of sentencing. You can critique each line for grammar, spelling, and punctuation as it appears before you.

Tip 4: *Let it set.* If possible, let your typed drafts or page proofs rest in a desk drawer for a few days. Later, you can proofread the copy with "new eyes." You will have forgotten the exact sequence you originally used in the written presentation and will now be able to judge it as an outside reader.

Have you ever discovered some of your old high-school or college theme papers several years after graduation? Embarrassing, aren't they? Ah, if you only could have judged them then with the cold eye of time you now have. The same principle applies to what you are currently writing. Let it get cold, then analyze it.

Tip 5: *Juxtapose pages*. As long as the pages of a twenty-page short story are numbered, there's no reason you can't shuffle them. Each page can then be analyzed as one unit and you won't be distracted by your concentration on the overall content.

Tip 6: *Vary the routine*. If you find your desk burdened with galleys from your latest book, typed draft copy for your next book, and a final draft typed version of an article you've just completed, don't blitz through everything in rapid succession. Break it up. Read and approve the article and then relax and glance through your morning's mail. Read and critique the latest chapters in galley and then peruse a magazine. Vary the proofreading pattern. Keep alert and fresh for your proofreading.

Tip 7: *Consult outsiders*. Whenever you have the slightest doubt about a rule of grammar, punctuation, syntax, or spelling, use a reference source to check it. Your desk should have a dictionary, thesaurus, and a basic grammar handbook within easy reach. Other reference texts should be on your shelf nearby. If you use a word processor, programs capable of checking spelling can be purchased. You also can phone the "Grammar Hotline" at York College (Queens, NY) from 10 AM—4 PM (EST) Monday through Friday at (212) R-E-W-R-I-T-E for a telephone consultation.

Tip 8: *Assign helpers*. If you are absolutely too busy to see to it personally that your manuscripts are carefully proofread before they are sent to editors, hire a professional proofreader or rely on someone from your writers' club to help you. (Note: Some of the least expensive and most competent proof-readers are women who run freelance typing services out of their homes.)

To these eight tips you possibly can add others (such as always doing your own typing to *ensure* accuracy). These eight points, however, are all you really need to master in order to ensure that your manuscripts will praise, not bury you. Just remember that the proof is not in the pudding, it's in the reading.

A secondary, but important extra benefit, to careful proof-reading is the strengthening of the completed manuscript in regard to long-range marketing potential. An article that has been prepared in a superb fashion will often be something that can be resold many times on a cyclical rotation.

Cyclical Marketing

Once each year I really get on my wife's nerves. Rose is usually a loving wife and, for a fact, the best secretary I've ever had. But I know I've really pushed her to the limit when (usually around February) I hear her groan from her office, "Oh, no! Not *this* thing again. Aggghhh!"

The source of her agony is a manuscript of mine called, "How to Be an Effective Listener." Since 1978 I have sold that article to *Plus 60 Magazine, the Florida Real Estate Professional's Journal, Market Builder, Pace, Tucson Business Digest, Roto, New Cleveland Woman Journal, Editor's Workshop, Optical Management,* and to six newspapers. It also has appeared as part of my book *Uncommon Sense: Fueling Success Skills with Enthusiasm.*

And guess who has had to type it every time it was submitted somewhere? That's right: my faithful wife and secretary, Rose. The only thing that has preserved her sanity over the years is the knowledge that this one article has earned us thousands of dollars. (That's not to say, however, that she wasn't overjoyed when word processors came along and feature articles could be stored on discs and only the revisions in the article had to be retyped.) Remarketing favorite topics is a standard operational procedure of both writers and editors. Knowing about this can make your freelance marketing efforts very successful.

Faithful Old Standards

When King Solomon proclaimed three-thousand years ago that there was nothing new under the sun, he wasn't referring to magazine articles, but he could have been. The fact is, if you were to examine the back issues of the nation's leading magazines, you would discover that they have been covering the same topics over and over at regular intervals. True, the titles are different and so are the authors, but seldom the subjects.

The reason editors repeat articles is because audiences change. One year a young lady might subscribe to *Seventeen;* the next year, however, she'll switch to *Modern Bride;* the following year she's moved on to *Family Circle.* For a time your brother will read *Boy's Life;* he then will switch to *Hot Rod;* he'll finally wind up with *Gentleman's Quarterly.* As each magazine's audience rotates, it falls to the editors to replay the article topics which have earned each magazine its particular audience.

As a freelancer, this becomes important marketing knowledge for you. By studying back issues of a magazine which you wish to break into and thereby discovering its repetitive themes, you can project what its future rotational needs will be.

For example, let's assume that there is a magazine called *Big Time Investments* which pays 35 cents per word for articles. You want to make a sale there, so you go to the library and pull out the bound volumes of all editions of that magazine for the past six or seven years.

You begin to read the article titles in the tables of contents. As you do, you make a note of the generic topics it covers. Each time an issue runs an article about one of these topics, you make a check mark by it on your list (perhaps even noting the date it appeared).

At the end of your examination, your checklist perhaps reveals that *Big Time Investments* has run an article about diamonds every two years, an article about gold every eighteen months, an article about silver every year, an article about stocks every six months, and an article on real estate every other issue. So, you've now discovered the hottest general topic for this magazine: real estate.

Next, you carefully make a list of eight or ten of the article titles which relate to real-estate investments. You discover that three of the eight titles you've listed are these: "Buying Condos with No Downpayment"; "Full Financing for Rental Properties"; and "No Up-Front Cash for Eastern Land Tracts." This then tells you that the specific article topic which readers want covered most frequently is how to invest in real estate even if one lacks initial investment capital.

Knowing this, you next read all articles which *Big Time Investments* has published on that topic during the past five years. You take good notes. It isn't hard. You've found a dozen different articles on that topic, but after you've read four of them they've started to repeat themselves.

Dependable Magazine Topics Which Appear in Cyclical Intervals

Food: Recipes, Cake Designing, Specialty Desserts
Health: Diets, Exercise Programs, Vitamins, Sleep
Love: Dating, Marriage, Sex, Divorce, Widowhood
Family: Pregnancy, Childbirth, Adoption, The Elderly
Career: College, Interviews, Salary, Promotions
Money: Investments, Savings, Taxes, Estate Planning
Politics: Candidates, Laws, Lobbies, Investigations
Religion: Cults, Sects, Media Outreach, Prophecy
Entertainment: Travel, Hobbies, Athletics, Music
Fashion: Trends, Colors, Fabrics, Designs, Costs

Having analyzed your notes for the basic material needed for such an article, your next move is to find some sort of new angle for re-presenting it. There are three ways you go about this: (1) by getting quotes from experts on this topic who have not previously been featured in that magazine; (2) by developing unique sidebars, different photographs, and specialized graphics which give a "face lift" to this granddaddy topic's artistic layout in the magazine; and (3) by making sure that your article contains virtually anything new (previously unpublished) about this topic, such as new laws or regulations, current research and studies, and/or recently reported case histories.

You submit your feature, the editor recognizes it as exactly the thing his readers want, and he purchases it from you. He also sends you a letter and asks, "Have you ever written anything about the stock market?"

Naturally, you are only too eager to go back and discover what kind of stock market article has been most popular in *Big Time Investments* during the past five years. Once having discovered it, you prepare a new version of it, submit it, and once again please your editor.

Meanwhile, however, your original article (on no down-payment real estate) has been published in *Big Time Investments*. Because you sold first rights only, you now own the article again. You take your carbon copy from your file drawer, revamp it a bit to meet the editorial style of *Get Rich Tabloid,* and send it off. It sells a second time and you are convinced that you've written a standard which will be an annual sale for you for as long as your secretary can stand to retype it.

In fact, it occurs to you that you may rewrite your own article under a pseudonym three years from now and sell it to *Big Time Investments* again.

Modifying Book Contracts

Up to this point we have focused our attention primarily on article writing. Eventually, however, you will want to move on to the next logical phase of your writing career, that being the writing of books. In so doing, you should be prepared in advance to negotiate the terms of your first contract.

Most authors are so delighted to have a publisher accept their manuscripts for publication that they never dream of arguing any points in a "standard" book contract offered to them. But that's a mistake. It's the sure sign of an amateur and it's not good business.

Publishers are a lot like bankers. They are in business to

make as much profit as possible. In reality, without *you* neither the publisher nor the banker could exist. Nevertheless, they try to make you think that without *them, you* couldn't exist. That's ridiculous. But what is even more ridiculous is that most beginning writers (and borrowers) have started to believe that nonsense.

If you are new to contract negotiations, here are some tips to make you "street smart" in your next contract offer:

1. Unless the manuscript is a "work made for hire" agreement, the book should be copyrighted in the *author's name,* not the publisher's.

2. A clause should be added to the contract which will ensure that the publisher will at least consult the author regarding the design of the book's jacket.

3. A "Discontinuance of Publication" clause should specify that if the book goes out of print (usually determined by fewer than 250 sales per year), the author will be allowed to send a letter to the publisher asking for all publication rights to revert to the author. The publisher will then have 30 days to respond to the letter and six months to reissue the book; otherwise, publication rights return to the author.

4. A "Bankruptcy" clause should explain that if the publisher goes into bankruptcy, insolvency, reorganization, or dissolution, the publisher's rights to the author's book shall terminate.

5. A "Reservation of Rights" clause should reserve first serial rights to the author (because book excerpts are usually printed before the book is released). Second serial rights can be shared. Here is a model to use in this regard.

All rights in the Work now existing, or which may hereafter come into existence, not specifically herein granted, are reserved to the Author for his use at any time. Reserved publication rights include, but are not limited to, the right to publish or cause to be published in any form, excerpts, summaries and novelizations and dramatizations and motion pictures of the Work, thereof, not to exceed seventy-five hundred (7500) words in length, to be used for advertising and exploitation of motion pictures and televised motion pictures, or dramatizations based upon the Work.

6. An "Examination of Books of Account" should state that the author has the right (at his own expense) to examine the publisher's books insofar as they relate to sales of the author's books.

7. The matter of payment frequency should be open for discussion. If the publisher wants to pay just once a year and you want to receive royalties every thirty days, compromise at ninety-day or six-month payments. Some publishers have a computerized accounting system which cannot be modified. If so, go ahead and yield on this point as a trade-off item for something else.

8. A "Modification of Warranty" should state that if the publisher is sued regarding something in the author's book, the author not only will be able to choose his own defense lawyer, but shall also have approval rights on the lawyer(s) the publisher hires to defend the publishing company. Furthermore, if the publisher freezes the author's royalties until the case is settled, those payments must be sent to the author within 30 days after the court settlement.

9. An "Acceptability of Manuscript" clause should be worded something on this order:

Publisher shall notify Author within sixty (60) days of

its receipt of each manuscript as to its acceptability or nonacceptability. If in the sole opinion of the Publisher any one of the works is unacceptable to the Publisher, the Publisher shall provide the Author with a detailed list of reasonably required changes, and the Author shall have sixty (60) days from the receipt of said list to make such changes. If in the sole opinion of the Publisher the revised work is unacceptable to the Publisher, he may reject it by written notice within sixty (60) days of delivery of the revised manuscript.

10. If this is your second book (or more) for the same publisher, it would be best to insist upon separate royalty statements for each book. It can be worded this way:

Statement of Account

The Publisher shall not combine statements for other Works with the statement for this Work. Payments then due shall accompany such statements. Statements shall include the following information:

a) The number of copies printed and bound in the first printing and in all subsequent printings of each edition, the date of publication, and the retail price.

b) For each royalty rate, the number of copies sold, the number of copies returned, the amount of current royalties, and the cumulative totals.

c) The number of copies distributed gratis for publicity purposes, subsidiary rights purposes, or other purposes, the number remaindered, destroyed, or lost.

d) A description of all subsidiary rights payments in which the Author's share amounts to one hundred dollars ($100.00) or more, including the gross amount received for each license granted by Publisher, together with a statement of the percentage of the total payment which the Author's share represents.

11. Finally, the elements of "Subsidiary Rights Licenses" should be spelled out as specifically as possible. Here is one way:

a) The sale and/or license of all subsidiary rights shall be subject to the Author's written consent, such consent not to be unreasonably withheld.

b) Executed copies of all licenses where the Author's share of the proceeds exceeds one hundred dollars ($100.00) shall be forwarded to the Author within thirty (30) days from the making thereof.

c) Any license granted by the Publisher to reprint the Work in book club or paperback editions, or in any other medium except newspapers and periodicals, must explicitly prohibit the licensee from inserting advertisements in its edition of the Work without the written consent of the Author. The Publisher must also explicitly prohibit the licensee from causing any alterations in the text from the original hardcover version without first obtaining the written consent of the Author.

d) The Author's share of such rights income, less any unearned advances, shall be paid to the Author, at the Author's request, within thirty (30) days following the Publisher's receipt thereof.

Allow me to explain one set of circumstances wherein these rules will not apply so stringently. Unlike the secular publishers, most denominational publishing houses will have established practices related to copyright ownership and royalty payment rates. Seldom will they be open to changes in these set norms. There are good reasons for this: Unlike secular publishers, denominational publishers are primarily interested in publishing books that will fulfill a ministry of proclaiming the tenets most closely allied with the religious beliefs of that denomination. That is, denominational publishers focus primarily on a book's "mission" and "message" rather than its profit potential. The reverse is usually true in the secular publishing houses.

Of course, even denominational publishers have to pay for their employees, overhead costs, and publishing expenses. The writers who write for them understand this. They usually share the denominational publisher's chief goal of wanting to produce books with a special message and, as such, are willing to make contract concessions.

To this end, royalty rates may be (by necessity) lower than rates paid by secular publishers; royalty payments may also be made only once each year, rather than quarterly (to curtail extra bookkeeping costs); and copyright ownership may be shared by the publisher and the author (so that the publisher will have a fair and proper opportunity to hold onto and share in the earnings of those books which do prove to be profitable). Should you choose to write for a denominational publisher, be sensitive to the totally different reason it has for existing, that is, proclamation not profits.

In any sort of negotiations—with secular or denominational publishers—remember that the book is the creation of the author. As such, before turning it over to a publisher, elements of mutual gratification should be agreed upon and not dictated by one party or the other.

Writing a book is hard work. The author should be satisfied with the terms of compensation he or she receives.

—Dennis E. Hensley

3

Enhancing Your Writing

You've often been told that if you learn to apply the basics of good writing, you will improve your writing style. But what actually is writing *style?*

Style is not easy to define, yet it's the one writing element that most often determines acceptance or rejection by editors. Because of the variety of writing styles, it's especially difficult to explain what style is in reference to your own writing. Over the years, I have heard and read many definitions of writing style and, in one way or another, all were pretty accurate.

• Style is the ability to wrap up all your knowledge into a neat, concise package of writing.

• Without style, a manuscript is only so much research and information strung together.

• Sometimes style is nothing more than finding the simple or direct approach to a topic.

• Style is what you recognize as clarity after you've rewritten what you've written.

• Style is like magic. A good writer can make anything interesting, but a great writer can make it magical. That magic is a writer's individual style. And the magic—the style—is what is marketable.

- Style is nothing more than "having a way with words." It might sound simple, but it most certainly is not.
- Style is what you get when you stop thinking of writing as just an intellectual exercise and start thinking of it as an emotional journey into the world. That's when your writing will open up and pour out, and that's when you'll also find success in the marketplace.
- Style is the ability to make research readable.
- Style is when a writer finds his own voice and tells his story in his own way.
- Style is like a river—a constant flow of words and feelings, and whatever else, emotionally, mentally, gets pulled along the way.

None of these statements technically defines writing style. Individual style must come from one's own efforts and diligence in combining all of the many processes needed in order to develop a manuscript. Your particular way of combining the processes will set you apart from other writers. That individuality can be referred to as your style.

Stylistic quality and editorial depth are necessary for the success of any publication. If you want to be a published writer, you will need to develop a writing style that is appealing to editors and readers alike. There is only one sure way to develop an excellent style of writing—by writing and rewriting.

Before your manuscript is sent to market, it must be reworked carefully to make sure it has less the appearance of a threadbare carpet and more the fascination of an Oriental rug. It must have a quality style. It must be polished, because polishing is a way of enhancing a manuscript's content—and your writing style.

While many writers believe there is strength in length, most editors concur with Shakespeare that "Brevity is the soul of wit." But acceptable length is determined by the readers, as the success of every piece of writing ultimately is. Editors might be the connection between writer and readers, but success comes, always, with the style of a writer and the acceptance of that style by the readers. Readers don't know or care who an author's editor is; most readers can't even remember which company published the best book they ever read. That's unimportant to them. However, what *is* most often remembered and discussed about a best-seller is the beautiful style or the powerful way in which the author told the story. As such, style also serves as a marketing tool for the author.

It's good to keep in mind as you research, develop, and write the final draft of your manuscripts that the general objectives of all publications are to inform, influence, inspire, educate, entertain, and present information with style.

A style that was acceptable twenty years ago, however, may not be acceptable today. For example, today effective Christian communication need not use scientific vocabulary and a point of view of the scientific world. Writers can develop their articles and stories for Christian publications by using their imagination, imagery, poetry, and appeal to the intuition rather than to the logic of their subject. A magazine that many years ago presented all its editorial in a scientific way may today consist of editorial that is anecdotal and more lively, completely different in style. It's a good idea to read current issues of publications before you try to write for them; you can study their editorial style and write your manuscripts accordingly.

The style in your query letter is equally important. Considering how many queries an editor receives in one week, it makes sense to develop one with enough professionalism to make it exceptional. The key to selling your idea will come from the style in which your query is written. Many markets require a query first, so your initial letter may be the only chance you'll have to sell your idea to an editor.

Colorful phrases in your query will entice an editor. For example, I wanted to write an article about the wildflower season at Joshua Tree National Park. If you are writing about mountainsides fully blooming with wildflowers, you might use the phrase "cascade of color" to describe the flowers. It was that very description, in my query letter to the editor of *Los Angeles Times,* that sold an article idea. Make what you're selling become *vivid* through your words. Other writers also will have the same idea you have, but the syntax of your query, offering something different and a promise of style, is what will make your letter stand out among the rest.

Another example is this paragraph, which is the opening section of a query letter about Jimmie Heuga:

> You won't find the word "reanimation" in the dictionary. It's a concept that former Olympic skier Jimmie Heuga developed after he was diagnosed as having multiple sclerosis fifteen years ago. "At first the disease robbed me of my self-image," Heuga says. "Then I decided I wouldn't let it defeat me. I worked to become healthier and stronger—physically, mentally, sexually. I 'reanimated' my entire life."

"Reanimation" is a vivid word, and the preceding quote was taken from the interview. Heuga could have said, "I learned how to live again," but, instead, he used a much more active and vivid way to describe how he had fought the disease. The query promised a style which would be carried through in the manuscript. The article sold because Heuga, the vivid quote, sprightly query letter, and style in which the manuscript was written, appealed to the editor.

Isaac Asimov once said that the best professional advice he ever received came from an editor who returned some sample chapters and asked Asimov, "Do you know how Hemingway said that the sun rose in the morning?" Asimov replied, "No, how?" The editor said, "Hemingway said 'the sun rose in the morning.'" Asimov then proceeded to develop a similar sparse style. He's known for it today. Hemingway's style was direct and lean, but it was very powerful. It was perhaps the finest example of powerful writing, offering readers quick and entertaining reading. Maybe that's why it is so widely imitated by other writers today.

Specifics About Style

Don't use clichés and platitudes when you write. Delete all unnecessary adjectives and adverbs since these are only "word count increasers" which tend to clutter your writing style. The word *very* is one such word. Use it with restraint.

Remove repetitious words and phrases. For example, a "dark night" is "night." Period. A heated hot tub is either a hot tub or a heated tub. Why should it be both?

Change weak or passive verbs into strong, active verbs. In your rewriting you will find weak verbs easily. Don't say "hit" when "slapped" or "tapped" is more explicit.

Replace obscure words with common, easily understood, words. Don't try to impress readers with your vocabulary. (Many novice writers use obscure and big words after discovering them in the dictionary while searching for the spelling of another word.)

Eliminate exaggerations and biased opinions. Personal

emotions are all right for a personal experience article, but they have almost no place in a factual piece of nonfiction.

Rewrite unclear syntax or complex syntax into clear and simple syntax. This is important. Don't muddy your sentences with phrases that are written solely to shock or impress; instead, present your reader with an obvious message.

Word choice is an important element in developing your writing style. Use picture nouns when possible. It makes a difference. For example, is the "house" you're writing about or a shack or a mansion? Let the reader *see* it by choosing the one word which describes it best. The right noun will make a difference.

Use specific verbs. For example, did the man run, or jog, or skip?

Vary sentence length and structure. If all sentences contain the same number of words, it slows the pace. It also gets boring. And don't be afraid to break rules a bit by using one-word action sentences. Style permits the bending of grammar. A bit.

Do you want to entertain or to inform? You should be willing to work hard enough to develop a style and a manuscript that will do both.

If you are writing a story that calls for the use of flashbacks, be sure to put them in chronological order. Nothing is more difficult, but nothing confuses a reader more than flashbacks that are disorganized and difficult to follow.

Try to keep the key points of your article visible throughout the manuscript. Don't go off on tangents or sidetracks. Don't just use adequate examples, use the best you can find through research. Keep the vocabulary simple. This advice comes from all of the best-known authors. Fancy, obscure words may work for highly technical writing, but simple is sweet for most publications.

Never forget that the main thing you want to do is communicate. Get your idea across.

Write tightly. Reduce "along the lines of" to "like"; reduce "in the neighborhood of" to "about"; reduce "for the reason that" to "because." Keep your writing crisp and to the point.

A casual style of writing includes plenty of anecdotes, quotes, and dialogue as well as shorter words and sentences and an almost colloquial tone.

A lively style consists of short, pithy sentences. It appeals to the five senses, evokes emotion, and gives specific details. It includes vivid verbs, a variety of clauses and phrases, and figurative language. The writing is more graphic, more alive (hence, a "lively" style). Most feature writing is done in this style, and many profiles use a lively style which is heavy on quotations.

An anecdotal style is similar to a lively style. It is quick writing that provides a sprightly offering of information to readers. Today's readers enjoy reading about other people; so, the anecdotal style is preferred by many kinds of publications.

A factual style is not very colorful, but its material is presented crisply and with an obvious sense of flow and organization for the overall development of the article.

A compact style uses fewer words and often has a better chance of selling. Many publications today specifically feature fast-read articles and stories. An example I read early in my career is one I have never forgotten and especially remember when I'm tempted to put nonworking words in my manuscripts. A beginning writer was instructed by her editor to use fewer words in her articles. Her next article read, "Mr. Smith struck a match to see if there was gasoline in the tank. There was. Age 32."

Feature Writing

Lively feature writing is usually written in the present. Instead of writing "he said" or "she opened the door" or "they laughed," write "he says," "she opens the door," and "they laugh." Feature writing is timeless, so make it move in the present tense. Don't bog it down in the past. Make it alive.

Articles, novels, short stories, poems, nonfiction books filled with energy are those written in the active tense. The energy is there. We can feel it.

During a conference lecture, I was trying to explain this energy I often feel in manuscripts and the importance of active, timeless writing style. Stella Stone, a Michigan freelancer, later told me, "Well, it happened in the past, so I wrote it in the past. But I didn't have to, did I? Maybe that's why my manuscript hasn't sold." Just because something happened in the past, or your story takes place in the past, doesn't mean you have to write it in the past tense or the passive voice. Try to rewrite some of the manuscripts you haven't sold—bring them into an energy-filled active tense. You'll be surprised how you will improve the style and improve the marketability by using the active voice.

Style is absolutely necessary for quality in nonfiction, fiction, and poetry. An excellent salable topic can fail because of poor writing style, or, worse, lack of writing style. Sometimes style can be achieved by stretching the language, infusing new words, or using old words in new ways. Several years ago, I wrote a letter to the editor of a national magazine regarding a short story I had read in a current issue. I used the expression, "It was a marvelous read." After the editor printed my letter in his Letters column, I was immediately put on the rack by that magazine's readers as well as the *Writer's Digest* readers for using "read" as a noun. And most especially since I was editor of *Writer's Digest,* "the magazine that's supposed to teach writers how to use the language properly." Using "read" as a noun was outrageous, they claimed. Shame on me! Yes, everyone knows "read" is a verb, but it was the best word to use to express just what I wanted to express and was much more active. And it was, and still is, the best "read" I've known.

What's in a Word?

For more ways to improve writing style, think of the word *said*. It is as much overused today as it has always been. Writers on one hand are told to just use "said" if that's what they mean. But then, someone mentioned that it was OK to use "note," so instead of "Mary said," we now see far too many times "Mary noted." One simple method concerning dialogue and using "said" is letting Mary help you with the style of your writing. Mary can admit, blurt, insist, and mutter. Mary can do one of countless substitutes for "said." This is an ongoing issue in short-story and feature writing, in which quotations are readily used.

In June, 1966, *Writer's Digest* published a one-page reference that has proved invaluable to me for many years. Written by Alma Boice Holland, the one page offered fifty substitutes for "said." "Said" is editorially acceptable in manuscripts requiring dialogue, but why not improve your style and add drama, color, and life to an article or story by using other verbs? Holland suggested the following, among others: "It isn't true," he *shouted* (excitement). "It isn't true," he *in-*

sisted (frustration). "It isn't true," he *challenged* (argument). "It isn't true," he *gasped* (shock). Of course, one can't overdo the use of substitute verbs and allow them to be obtrusive to the reader, so sometimes it's better to use the simpler, "he said." Nevertheless, in developing your writing style, try to use some of the following alternatives: asked, admitted, blustered, boasted, complained, cried, defended, emphasized, hinted, invited, interrupted, mimicked, observed, persisted, prompted, philosophized (that's a great one), reasoned, repeated, scolded, teased, and whispered. What wonderful choices to improve our writing. And you'll find more if you spend some exploring time with your dictionary. I often use this dictionary search as a game to ward off writer's block.

One of the reasons manuscripts get rejected is that time and time again writers are careless about the words they've chosen and, as such, they don't express what they really mean. Be sure you know exactly what you're saying and how it sounds in the editor's mind. When we come right down to it, plain English is still better than anything else. We are, after all, writing to communicate. In down-to-earth, good, solid English write so that an editor can understand and readers can respond. Don't try to impress an editor with your fancy vocabulary. He won't like it. And his readers will never get a chance to read it. Flashy, obscure words won't work. Unless the vocabulary is natural to your style—smooth and easily understood—it won't be impressive.

A finely polished style is a style that is found in a clean, professional manuscript. Part of style enhancement is accurate spelling and checking to make certain that all proper names and figures in the manuscript are accurate. For example, if the subject of your interview is age thirty-seven and your error goes to an editor who trusts your accuracy, how would your work as a writer stand up if you carelessly typed the subject's age as seventy-three? It might go unnoticed by everyone except your interviewee, but it's doubtful. I have seen manuscripts that have spelled one person's name four different ways. In other manuscripts the name was not spelled correctly in any instance. Correct spelling is always important, but never as important as the proper spelling of someone's name. Editors immediately distrust everything else you've written in a manuscript if you haven't spelled a person's name properly or given his age accurately.

When you're in a rush—stop. Wait until you don't need to be in a hurry, because rushing results in far too many errors. The following cover letter accompanied an unsolicited manuscript which was sent to me as an editor at *Writer's Digest:* "I hope you like my enclosed manuscript. I have been very careful to make sure all the words are spelled correctly and the manuscript is properly *punctured.*" Luckily for the writer, her manuscript was not hurriedly written, and we ultimately decided to buy it. Most editors wouldn't be so tolerant, however. Manuscripts can't be dashed off. Style takes time.

Grammar is another consideration when developing good writing style. You need not be a slave to grammar, however. Clarity is important above all other considerations. Still, this is not to say that rules of grammar can be ignored.

The best advice about grammar comes from author Gary Provost, in his article, "Ain't You a Little Too Concerned About Good English?" (WD, May 1984):

> Good writing and good grammar are not twins, but they are usually found in the same places. The rules of grammar exist to help you write well, not to sabotage your work, and you cannot write well without them. They organize the language

just as the rules of arithmetic organize the world of numbers. Imagine how difficult math would be if 3 and 3 only equalled 6 once in a while or if a tenth was only equal to 10 percent when somebody felt like it. Rules of grammar exist so that we can all communicate well.

How we communicate is part of our individual writing style. Poor grammar is confusing. Good grammar helps your writing sing. We've heard about poets who can only write poetry that is to be read aloud, because when read silently, the poems don't sing. Articles written with the rules of grammar in mind sing, while bad grammar makes them seem to be out of tune.

Charles Dickens knew what style was and used it as well as any writer in history, but more important than his knowledge of style was his ability to present the style clearly, through the use of good grammar, to his readers. "When I read your story about Little Nell, I cried," said one woman to Dickens. "When I wrote the story of Little Nell, I cried," replied the famous author.

Most of us want to develop a clear writing style. From his book, *The Techniques of Clear Writing,* Robert Gunning gives us the following advice which will keep our "fog index" down. The fog index is a useful tool for measuring readability. It can help you improve your writing style and make your manuscripts ring with clarity. Keep sentences short, twenty words or fewer. Prefer the simple to the complex. Avoid unnecessary words (make every word carry its weight). Put action in your verbs. Write the way you talk—conversational tone is always best. Use terms your reader can picture and concrete words that stand for things you can see and touch and feel. Tie in with your reader's experience along the way; put yourself in the reader's place; bring the reader into the article or story. Use *you* often. Use variety and fresh forms of expression. Write to express, not to impress. Don't show off. Make your ideas clear. Exclamation marks and italics don't improve your writing style. Correct punctuation does, however, so it's best to read your manuscripts out loud before submitting them. If something has to be italicized, find a simpler way to write it without the italics or exclamation points. For clarity, keep sentences and paragraphs short. Quotes and conversational dialogue add warmth and intimacy to articles and stories. If you use statistics, dramatize them or make someone say them, don't just list numbers.

Use of quotations brings life to an otherwise dry presentation of facts and ideas. Told in the words of characters in a story, or authorities in an article, transitions are made easier and more effectively through the use of quotations.

Getting Organized

Organization of material is another important element of writing style. Aside from writing the lead, the middle, the statement of purpose, and the closing, other elements of organization are also needed. Each writer develops his or her own habits of organization. Perhaps by explaining my system to you, you'll pick up some ideas to assist your own organizational processes. I'm explaining my method of organization not to suggest it's the only way but that it is *a* way. It works for me. It's a method I developed during the twenty or more years I've been writing.

First, I type everything loosely from notes and ideas I have written on scraps of paper and from my random thought-jotting. I always remember that the more tightly I organize the research material, the easier the writing will go. Fewer drafts will be needed. I type all the information, page after page, in no kind of order, no sense of story flow or progression. Later, I prepare a detailed outline from memory. I ask myself, what is the article about? How will it be developed? What kind of article flow will be the best approach? Then I type up an outline. I organize all my typed material. Outlining is the key to organization. Without a solid outline there's no way to know what goes where, what follows what, what goes first, second, and last.

After I've gotten everything on paper, I photocopy all the pages, mark them "original research" and file them. I sit in the middle of the floor with scissors, cellophane tape, and blank paper. I go through my typed notes, paragraph by paragraph, marking in the margins the main subject of each paragraph. I also jot "possible lead" or "strong closing" if I read a quote or some facts that make me believe such material is suitable for a good lead or closing. I organize all paragraphs into some kind of commonality, then I smooth out the transitions as I organize each subject into even more definite sections. Next, I paper clip each subject/theme together, after reading them as a whole unit and putting them into organized stacks according to flow and transitional possibilities. Finally, I put all the stacks of paragraphs into a semblance of order, according to my outline.

My Rod McKuen interview, for example, which appeared as the cover story of the February 1984 issue of *Writer's Digest,* when transcribed, ran 120 pages. However, the length for WD only called for twenty-five pages. Talk about a job of intense organization! I did a lot of honing for that project. Organization is difficult when you have too much good, usable material, and you want to share it all with readers. It takes some restraint and common sense, and a thorough knowledge of your audience.

Once you have your material outlined and organized, you must consider transitions which will carry the reader from one point to another smoothly, efficiently, unobtrusively. Step back from whatever you've just written. Act as though you're saying, "OK, this is where I've been, now here's where I plan to go next." Offer contrast. "This is how it was, but here's how it's going to be."

Word pivots are the most often used transitions. They work as links in a chain of paragraphs (*and, but, thus, in comparison,* and so forth). Just don't overdo them. Word repetition (listening for the echo of one paragraph) is another technique. It's difficult to master but an effective way to bring the readers to the next part of your manuscript.

Usually, you can sense a rough transition when you read an article. It makes you ask, "How did I suddenly get here?" So, when you read your final drafts, read carefully to be certain you have smooth transitions throughout, and correct those areas which seem rough to you. They won't be difficult to locate in your manuscript—they seem to "announce" themselves.

Writing Effective Leads

The lead is where your article lives or dies. It should excite readers. So watch your words. Write to be read, not to be deciphered. Readers won't take time to work hard at understanding what you've written. Editors won't either.

Writing the lead can be sheer agony. If you don't grab the reader in the lead, you will lose him forever. Sometimes we think we'll never get the manuscript written, but somehow we always do, and usually the lead is the most difficult part to write.

A lead is like a sideshow barker offering a promise of the

reward and pleasure to come, a pacesetter and moodsetter for the story that follows. A lead must draw readers into the article or story by enticing them. And a good lead can excite a reader.

Editors know how crucial a lead can be. It has to be clear, provocative, valid, vigorous, or shocking. The mood and manner of the lead should match the mood of the article or story. For example, a frivolous lead should not precede a serious article.

"Words," wrote Robert Southey, an early nineteenth-century English poet, "are like sunbeams; the more they are condensed the deeper they burn." So brevity is best for a lead style. Ten words comprise the lead in the world's best-seller: "In the beginning God created the heaven and the earth."

A good lead points the way to a good closing. It teases the reader into the story, whereas a closing emphasizes the point of the story.

Why does a lead fail? A number of reasons can be cited: It may be dull, written like every other story before it, offering nothing exciting and new to the reader. It may have too many details which bore the reader. It may be too long. This is what editors mean when they say, "It takes too long to get into the article." Every word in your lead should be exact and necessary. A poor lead might contain pointless anecdotes. Writers hear that a good lead can be anecdotal, so they jam inapplicable anecdotes into their leads. Stiff or unnatural dialogue is another reason leads fail.

A lead can be one word or one paragraph, or it can be four good paragraphs, so you can be flexible in writing the length of your leads. First ask, "Why should the readers care?" That's the question your lead has to answer.

Here are different approaches for writing effective leads:

The News Summary Lead uses the *who, what, where, when, why,* and *how* technique of writing an article. Most often used by daily newspapers, the summary lead caters to readers who skim the newspaper, searching for fast news.

If you're stumped on writing your lead, here's a suggestion that might help: jot down the five *Ws* and *H,* fill in brief facts for each, and usually you will have something factual to use in your lead. Or think of your lead as a kind of press release. Get all the abbreviated facts introduced quickly, then write the body of your article and expound on those facts.

The Quotation Lead might be used if you're short of strong copy for your lead. The quotation might come from literature, poetry, or history. Whatever the source, it should be relevant to the article and provide an opportunity to make a smooth and logical transition from the quotation into the body of the article. Clever use of quotations always provides a good lead. Being a quotation collector for many years, I believe everyone likes a strong, provocative, or humorous quotation from a known celebrity, famous personality, or respected authority.

The Capsule Lead is an abbreviated form of the news summary lead, usually less than one printed line long. Often it contains just two or three words, packed with power. For example, "President Nixon has resigned" or "Winter weather is returning."

The Simple-Statement Lead, sometimes called "The Stage Setter," distills the facts and the mood of a story into a direct statement. For example, "American motorists are getting edgy again," for an article on the fuel shortage.

The Quote Lead works best when you're writing an interview or profile of a celebrity. This type of lead is always popular and sometimes overdone, but people like to read about people, and starting with a strong or lively quote is a dependable grabber lead.

The Tabular Lead can be used when your research has provided you with far too many facts—all of them interesting and many of equal importance. Write quick, simple sentences, stringing these facts together. This is an unusual kind of lead, but effective if the material is available.

The Question Lead is an old standby, often used when there is no other possible way to write a lead. Ask a question in your lead to arouse curiosity. Provide the answer in the copy that immediately follows. The beauty of this kind of lead is the ease of transition that follows.

The Dialogue Lead can be used if you're writing about a colorful personality or a suitable and lively subject, and you have a wealth of notes or tapes of verbal exchanges. It's lively and attractive to editors as well as to readers. This lead contains four or five short paragraphs of active dialogue such as questions and answers between yourself and the person being interviewed.

The Striking-Statement Lead is similar to the Simple-Statement Lead, but violent, startling, perplexing, shocking, or astonishing. For example, "Mother Nature, you're under arrest," for an article about unusually calm weather.

The Descriptive Lead is a vivid word picture of the subject, the site, or a situation. It draws the reader to the place and quickly creates interest in the subject. Your research should easily tell you if this lead is right, depending on the material you have available.

The Narrative Lead uses anecdotes and the storytelling arts of the fiction writer. It's an informal and entertaining lead.

The narrative lead and the anecdotal lead are one in the same.

The Contrast Lead, or Comparison Lead, offers dramatic contrast of two obviously different facts, comparing the then and now, or using other forms of analogy.

The First-Person Lead, though rarely used, is possible, depending on the purpose and significance of the message and on the writer. Obviously, for a first-person article, it's a natural lead.

The Direct-Address Lead is a strong direct statement. It's a lead which seems to snap its fingers in front of the face of the reader without preaching or scolding them. It is most often used in service articles and survey articles.

The Freak Lead is not appealing, but sometimes used by publications which like to use typographics devised to attract reader attention. A visual "catch" for the readers' eyes. These are weak leads, and should be avoided.

The Teaser Lead can be found in almost every good lead. Present the facts and slant of your article in a teasing style, almost like a minigame for readers.

The Hybrid Lead is a combination of two or more of all the other types of leads. It is difficult to write. The most successful hybrid lead is a combination of the Question Lead with the Quotation Lead. For example, "Who said it would be easy?" asked John Doe. "I did," replied Mary Smith.

If you're like most writers, when you finish writing a satisfactory lead, you can move on to writing the body of the article or story. Some writers write the body first, then struggle to develop a strong lead. However you work, the lead is important enough to spend as much time with as necessary to make it outstanding. Your lead should be the best you have to offer.

Writing Memorable Closings

Although strong leads and good story organization and development are extremely important to a successful writing style, the closing of an article or story is often the most memorable part of anything you write. You must learn to provide a memorable finish, otherwise everything that goes before the closing will be mentally laid aside by the readers. They might even wonder why they bothered to read your article at all. The closing should give readers something to take away with them, to keep, remember, and share, like a gift.

We don't write just to tell a story, we write so that the story will be remembered by the readers. And that happens in the closing, not in the lead or in the body. An article begins with a theme, an idea, or a slant. That idea is developed point by point in the body, but it is in the conclusion, or closing, that we show our most creative work. Writing the closing isn't easy. It comes after keen thinking and planning. Always note good closing material as you go through your research during organization of the article. You must choose your closing paragraph wisely.

Good writers believe that the opening and closing should wrap up the middle. How often we hear or read that the logical progression of any good piece of writing is "beginning, middle, end; lead, body, close." The closing should tie a ribbon around the rest of the article. In a way, you're telling the reader, "Well, now, here's what I've told you, and here's what I think you should remember."

There are no magic formulas, but here are a few suggestions for developing good closings:

The Quotation Close ends with an appropriate quotation.

What is quoted either succinctly summarizes the article or adds an element of humor or irony to what has been explained.

The Lead Replay is a duplication or rewrite of the lead, with some amplification. Sometimes the author can simply repeat the article's lead statement.

The Restatement of Purpose of your article provides a vivid or lively restatement of that purpose. It helps the reader reach the article's logical conclusion.

The Add-On is an unusual closing technique, because it makes a point that has not been made in the article or story. It can be a shocker or a bit of news that fits nicely as a wrap-up closing statement.

The Proximity Close is developed by closely reading the material preceding your final paragraph to discover a closing angle. Then summarize that material or statement and make the closing one strong, brief statement that capsulizes the penultimate paragraph of your article.

A Play on Words, or alliteration, makes a vivid impression and stays with the readers. It's a tricky closing to write, however, so don't get too cute with it or it might not work.

The Anecdotal Closing is good, but sometimes difficult to develop effectively. You can close with a complete anecdote or use a split anecdote, telling part of an anecdote earlier in the article, then using the balance of that anecdote for the closing.

The Summary Closing distills highlights of the article or ties up all the loose ends. It often points back to the lead or seems like a summarizing overview of what has been presented.

The Stinger Closing is an unexpected conclusion, startling, surprising, shocking to readers. Although it jolts the reader, it nevertheless must make sense within the context of the article.

The Natural Closing might sound like it's easy to write, but it's tough. You let your story end "naturally." You tell your story, then stop. It's rare when an article's progression will supply this kind of natural closing.

The Straight-Statement Closing is also called the assessment or editorial closing. It consists of a few sentences or final thoughts about the subject, in your own words, which are not redundant of what you wrote earlier in the article. It is not a summary, seldom is long-winded, and generally is short and right to the point you wish to make.

The Word-of-Advice Closing is one last warning or word of advice, a blunt but effective way to get one final, important point across. For example, "The next time you think about driving when you've been drinking—don't!" as the closing to an article about drunk drivers.

The Echo Ending uses some word or phrase or part of a quotation that has been repeated often and preeminently in your article. It weaves it into the closing in a meaningful, surprising, or clever way.

Closes and their approaches are fascinating challenges, but they can be frustrating. They are fascinating because they provide a strong means to inform, persuade, or affect your reader. They are frustrating because they can be the most difficult portion of an article to write.

Self-Editing

Perhaps the best way to improve your writing style—and for some writers, a way to actually discover it—is to try self-editing. Self-editing is the polishing and rewriting of an article, and it's the rewriting that you do after self-editing that enhances your style. There are several methods of self-editing.

First, give the manuscript distance. Work far in advance of your assigned or self-imposed deadline. Allow a day or two to set your manuscript on the back burner. Then return to it and begin self-editing:

Start with line editing. Check each line of your manuscript as it stands alone. Launder crude phrases, clichés, street jargon, hip talk, and slanderous statements and opinions. Check for ambiguity. Don't assume the readers know—a good writer never assumes anything—but the trick is not to write down to your readers, either. Change or improve word choices, and be certain of correct word usage. We laugh when Archie Bunker uses words in a dumb way, but editors don't like a careless attitude, and it is careless to use words incorrectly. Are there minor discrepancies in character and plot of your short story? Is the development of material full and the organization smooth in your article? This kind of scrutiny of your manuscripts will improve quality and raise the style of your writing to an acceptable level.

Writing and polishing a manuscript, and cutting it to length, takes time. It also takes time to develop an attractive writing style, but every writer knows it's worth it.

Powerful writing is packed with style and loaded with clarity. When editors are asked to describe their editorial needs, the most common statement is, "We need well-written material." "Well-written" is an overused term, but if a manuscript is written well, an editor knows it immediately. If it's written poorly, the manuscript fails to make it into the marketplace.

When editors talk about style, they refer to editorial style of their publications. When writers talk about style, they refer to the magic that makes their words sing clearly. But editorial style and writing style should complement each other; only then will writers and editors make a happy marriage for readers to enjoy.

—Rose A. Adkins

4

Fifteen Forms of Specialized Writing

Now having spent time teaching you how to write and market your manuscripts in a professional manner, I want to focus on the real emphasis of this book, the various forms of specialized freelance writing. Whereas it would be virtually impossible to discuss all the varieties of specialty writing in which freelance writers can become involved, my goal in this section is to concentrate on the fifteen writing specialties which have remained in constant demand over the years. We'll begin on an upbeat note by looking at humor and comedy writing.

Marketing Humor

People often ask me if I remember my first article sale. That's like asking Ike if he remembered D-Day.

My first money earned as a freelance writer was twenty-five dollars paid to me by *Military Life* for a one-paragraph humorous story based on my early days as a soldier. It went like this:

Working as a Chaplain's Assistant at the Fort Knox Reception Station, I got used to countless new recruits coming into my office with complaints on adjustments to Army life. One of the practices during this initial week the recruits spent at the station was to have each man "donate" a pint of blood. One afternoon a man came storming into my office yelling, "I can't take it! They cut off all my hair, took away my civilian clothes . . . I mean, what do they want from a guy— *blood?*" "Oh, no," I assured him. "That's not until tomorrow."

By paying attention to what was just naturally funny around me, I had earned twenty-five cents per word on my first sale. A month later I sent another hundred-word item to *Military Life*. It was based on funny signs seen around an Army post. It, too, earned me twenty-five dollars and a by-line. (In 1971, twenty-five cents per word was great pay, especially for a beginning freelancer. I've been known to humble myself even now to such wages. As often as possible, in fact.)

In 1972 I sold my first short story. It was a thousand-word humorous fantasy called, "Could Beethoven Have Made It in Nashville?" *Stereo* paid forty dollars for it. I had borrowed the idea from an argument Lucy had had with Schroeder (in "Peanuts") over the range of Beethoven's talents. Humor, I discovered, was all around me if I would just see it.

Today, I still turn to comedy and humor writing as a source of income and enjoyment. Here, for example, is a filler I had appear in the June 1982 issue of *Writer's Digest:*

Nom'n Clatters

What's in a name? If paraphrased, possibly a good book title. Here are a dozen titles that were overlooked by their authors:
The Suitmaker Was a Good Screamer by Taylor Caldwell
Fieldhouse Clergyman by Jim Bishop
Stealin' the Chef by Robin Cook

Tumbled Kewpie by Roald Dahl
Lift England's Capitol! by Jack London
Over the Center Field Wall by Homer
Sincere Seamstress by Ernest Hemingway
A Latrine Drifted to the Dam by John Updike
The Pork Christmas Ornaments by Hamlin Garland
Rice Tea by Saki
A Crazier 2,000-Pound Bramble by Thornton Wilder
A Sincere Expletive Killing by Frank G. Slaughter

If you are alert to humorous situations in life, you can generate all kinds of funny stories and articles. One of my writing students once handed in a term paper on the subject of violence in sports. His girlfriend had mistyped it as "Violins in Sports." I thought the title was hilarious. I couldn't wait to read the paper. Later, I was crushed to discover the title was a typo. So, I sat down and wrote the "Violins in Sports" article, suggesting that a string quartet should be available for dirge music at football games and boxing matches. It was satirical and really funny. It sold for fifty dollars the first time out.

If you've never tried your hand at humor writing, you should. Try your brain while you're at it, too. The subject areas are endless: world events, the human body, politics, UFOs, people's egos, automobiles, gardening, pollution, the generation gap, pets, modern music, contemporary fashions. Just pick up a daily newspaper and take off on anything you find there.

Humor can be expressed in a myriad of forms. You can experiment with comic relief, light humor, understatement, exaggeration, slapstick, drollness, wit, irony, absurdity, parody, spoofs, or satire. The great humorists of all time have created comedic scenes and lines which are timeless.

Mark Twain was a master of understatement. Throughout

A Connecticut Yankee his narrator lauds Sir Lancelot. Finally, at one point, with everyone knowing that Lancelot is virtually invulnerable, the newspaper reports, "Last Thursday in a local meadow, Sir Lancelot and the Brown Knight met in combat. The widow has been notified." (What more needs to be said, eh?)

Cervantes was brilliant at creating slapstick. I can still recall when I first read *Don Quixote*. When I got to the outrageous scene in which Quixote mixed together a magic elixir (composed of garbage) and forced it down his squire's throat, I guffawed out loud for five minutes. Poor Sancho Panza. What a scene! Hilarious!

The ingredient that turns a common event into something funny is the *point of view* the humorist gives it. In effect, he says to his readers, "But what if you looked at it this way?" The reader is then shown a situation from a perspective he never would have considered on his own. If it's funny, he'll laugh.

Recently, for example, there was a lot of press play about entertainers who were pooling their money to form large companies. So in a filler I sold I asked, "What if Rich Little, Liza Minelli and Jane Fonda went into business together? Their company would be called Little, Liza and Jane."

Note how humor is based on truth. Though exaggerated or satirized, its topic has a core which readers can identify with. Many times it uses standard expressions or common references to make it even more real for readers. This can help you in deciding what to have some fun with. Ask yourself basic questions:

(1) What aggravates me most and how can I explain it humorously?

(2) What are my spouse's/children's oddest habits and how can I explain them in a funny scene?

(3) What have I seen on TV lately that would be fun to parody?

(4) What outrageous things would happen if I were able to put two well-known, but incredibly different people together on a desert island?

Next, make notes about the subject. What age, size, shape, color, taste, or weight is associated with it? What behaviors, habits, traditions, rules, laws, or skills apply to it? From these notes, then see what happens when you apply the comedic formats to each item. For example, start with age. Is age in this case funny if it's exaggerated? understated? made a parody of in a similar situation? Just experiment and see what you come up with.

Eventually, when you've compiled enough funny one-liners, gags, funny scenes and satirical remarks, you can formulate them into one large article or story. It's worth the effort. There's good money to be made in writing humor. No joke.

Fillers and Short-Shorts

If you are a part-time freelance writer, you probably write in spurts. You dash off a few lines during lunch break, while the kids are down for a nap, or during the half hour while your spouse is looking at the news on television before bed.

If this profile fits you, you should consider concentrating your efforts on breaking into print via the filler and short-shorts markets.

Fillers are small humorous or informative items of fewer than 250 words. They include a recipe for *Virtue,* a funny story for *Reader's Digest,* a joke for *American Legion Maga-*

zine or a money management tip for *Christian Business Life Digest*. Payment for such items ranges from ten to four-hundred dollars, but an average payment is thirty dollars.

Short-shorts are miniarticles of 250 to 1,000 words which focus on one topic and offer opinions on it or information about it. Syndicated columnists such as James T. Kirkpatrick and Paul Harvey usually feature 750-word short-shorts for their columns. The short-short can earn payments ranging from twenty-five to a thousand dollars, but an average payment is about sixty-five dollars. The bonus value of writing short-shorts, however, is that they are easy to resell to a variety of markets. Thus, a short-short written during one lunch hour and sold ten times may gross six-hundred-fifty dollars in total return.

Editors enjoy it when freelancers send them a steady stream of articles of under a thousand words. They can be read and judged quickly. If purchased, they can be used to fill up odd half- or quarter-page spots in the issue being laid out. Besides that, editors know that readers like short articles that can be read quickly in a dentist's waiting room or during coffee breaks at work.

To write a filler or short-short, make a list of whatever you can discuss off the top of your head. It may be something nostalgic, a personal opinion about something, or a list of ways to do something more efficiently. Begin there. Write a brief article about whatever you know well. Keep it snappy, obvious, simple to follow, and concise (usually about three typewritten pages).

Be sure to touch on the things that will be of most importance to the reader: the benefits, the costs, the materials needed, the time involved, the people concerned. If you need specific data that you don't know offhand, check an almanac or encyclopedia for general information. For more current facts, either contact the U.S. Public Information Centers or check the *Encyclopedia of Associations* (Gale Research Co.) for an association that can answer your questions.

Keep your paragraphs tightly written and short. Use action verbs and picture nouns to make the copy strong. Eliminate any superfluous adjectives, adverbs, clauses, clichés, or redundancies.

Once your first draft is completed, go back through it and try to eliminate whole paragraphs if they refer to a tangent topic or offer one example too many. Stay on *one* topic. If things get too involved, break your longer feature into two short articles (past/present or people/products or cars/trucks, and so forth).

Virtually anything of interest as conversation qualifies as a potential topic to cover in a short-short. Here are some general categories:

(A) *Places* (unique restaurants, bizarre museums, factory tours, and so forth)

(B) *Hobbies* (cow riding, cartooning, marble shooting)

(C) *Marriage/Family Life* (teaching hubby to cook, teaching junior about his ethnic heritage)

(D) *Holidays* (Beating post-Christmas blahs, dyeing Easter eggs)

(E) *Book Reviews, Stage Screen Reviews*

(F) *Recipes, Crafts, Sewing Tips, Family Projects, Games*

(G) *Business Tips* (time management ideas, buying briefcases, and so forth)

(H) *Profiles* (life of a prison guard, struggles of a young evangelist)

Your primary markets for fillers and short-shorts will

be small-circulation magazines, newspaper Sunday supplements, company publications and general consumer periodicals. While recently cleaning out my file cabinets I discovered that in one year I had sold seventeen short-shorts to *Grit* newspaper, twenty-one short-shorts to the *Indianapolis Star Magazine,* and twenty-five fillers to various other publications. The topics ranged from a profile of a man who had a collection of company imprint seal makers to an outline of three off-the-beaten-path tourist attractions in Michigan's upper peninsula. Each of the short items had been written while I was employed full time as a college professor. They had been written in spurts, but had added seventeen-hundred dollars to my income that year.

And that's the long and short-short of it.

Topics for Fillers and Short-Shorts

Four Tips for Home Security
Reducing Postage Costs
Unusual Ways to Get to Work (skateboard, bike, helicopter)
How Employees Use Coffee Breaks
What the Company Logo Means
An Idea for Beating Job Boredom
It's Harder If You're Left-Handed
Six Easy Ways to Conserve Home Energy
Why I Refinanced My House
A Telephone Operator's Funniest Experience
Zany Office Regulations at Major Companies
Suggestions on How to Drive in Bad Weather
Our Week with a Foster Child
Five Ways Not to Fight the Common Cold

Statistics About Smoke Detectors
How to Probe a Flea Market
Why Americans Resisted Metric Changeovers
The Effect of Cheap Calculators on Teaching Math
Contemporary Office Jargon
Preparing for a Pregnancy Leave
Winter Home-Emergency Preparedness
Six Things We Can Feel Optimistic About
Is Early Retirement a Good Idea?
Local Speakers' Bureaus
Weekend Warriors: National Guardsmen on Duty

Specialty Book Reviews

It took me four years to research and write my doctoral dissertation. In the process, I became one of the six most knowledgeable people in the world on the life and writings of American author Jack London.

That may not impress you. It probably doesn't. Even my mother asked, "Jack who?" when I announced my dissertation topic back in 1976.

Nevertheless, each year I receive a phone call from some Hollywood television or movie producer asking me for some sort of information about London or about one of his books, or I receive letters from college students asking for my opinions on certain of London's works. Over the years I've been contracted by a West Coast publisher to write a book about Jack London and I've written seventeen major essays about London which have appeared in nine different well-known scholarly journals.

What this proves is that if you become an expert on

something—virtually anything—you'll find yourself in demand sooner or later. And since most of us have some sort of thing we are proficient at, we all eventually do have our day in the sun.

But have you ever considered the idea of not waiting for your day of recognition to come but, instead, of taking a step toward having that day become *today?* You can, you know. You can do it by becoming a specialty book reviewer.

General book reviews, like those found in your weekend newspapers, provide readers with a book's title, author, publisher, price, and length, as well as the reviewer's opinion of the plot, main characters, and author's writing style. Such reviews usually are about 150 to 225 words long and are designed to give the reader enough basic information so that he or she can decide whether or not to read the book.

Specialized book reviews are different. The specialized review appears only in periodicals which are read by a limited audience of people who have a common interest or similar careers. For example, *Insight* magazine is for optometrists, opticians, and people in the eye-care field; the only book reviews which appear in this magazine are reviews of books dealing with eyeglasses, contact lenses, artificial eyes, and eye-examination techniques. Similarly, *ShopTalk* is a magazine for cosmetologists; the only books it reviews are those which focus on hair styles or beauty shop management.

I recommend to beginning reviewers that they go to a large library and examine a variety of specialty journals, magazines, and tabloids. A list of four to six magazines should be made which cover whatever area the reviewer is already knowledgeable about. For example, if the reviewer had extensive knowledge of the insurance business, he or she could note that *Leader's Magazine, The Fielder, Market Builder, Pacesetter,* and *CLU Digest* all use reviews of books which cover insurance sales, laws, or agency operations.

The next step is to write a letter of introduction to the magazine's managing editor. In the letter, outline your level of education, your years of professional experience, and your list of previous writing credits. Enclose two sample reviews (one 150 words long, one 650 words long) of books in the field of the magazine's interest. Explain to the editor that you are available to start preparing reviews as soon as the editor might want to forward a book to you. (Book publishers send free copies of their newly released books to editors of periodicals. The editors then decide which books they want reviewed in their magazine. Those selected books are then sent to the magazine's reviewers.)

Payment for a specialized book review usually consists of allowing the reviewer to keep the book, a small honorarium (ten to forty dollars), and a byline on the printed review. No one gets rich by writing specialized book reviews, but many people are able to keep up with their reading this way while also amassing a large collection of first-edition books at no cost. Quite often, a freelance consultant will become a specialized book reviewer just for the benefit of keeping his or her name before the people who use his services. It's free advertising directly to a prime target market.

It is important to analyze the magazine you plan to write for so that your book review will match the style, length, and content focus of other material found in the periodical. Every publication has its idiosyncrasies that must be recognized. Some editors forbid off-color language to appear in a review, even if it's a direct quote from the book. Some editors want the review to contain a sample passage from the book. Each publication has its preferences. Learn them and don't go against the norm.

When you read a book for review, keep colored pencils or markers close at hand. Underline key sentences and paragraphs in red, interesting examples or anecdotes in blue, and humorous items in green. Mark comments to yourself in the margins which you can later refer to when writing the review.

In writing your specialized review, you must be sure to include answers to these questions:

(1) What are the author's credentials for writing this book?

(2) How in-depth was the research upon which the book is based?

(3) How does this book relate in theme and/or quality to the author's earlier books?

(4) Which ideas presented in this book are new; which are not?

(5) Did the author accomplish what he or she intended to do in the book?

In offering your opinion of the book's merit, do not be swayed by a publisher's publicity material, a flashy cover, or a list of praiseworthy quotes supposedly gathered from other critics and reviewers. Go with your own gut instincts—how would you feel about the book if you had *paid* for a copy?

Be original in your expressions. Stay away from press hype ("a breakthrough in science writing," "a great new talent on the scene"). Avoid generalities; instead, be point-blank in saying where the book succeeds or fails.

If editors and readers can learn to value your review judgments, you will always have a following and a reading audience. And remember this: each time you read a new book in your specialty area, you are adding to your own range of competence. You benefit, the reader benefits, and the periodical benefits.

That's a combination hard to beat.

Guest Editorials

One of the advantages of living in a society which permits freedom of speech and press is the chance to "sound off" about matters that irritate or please you. One of the most effective ways of doing this is by writing a guest editorial for your local newspaper or a national magazine. Not only do you get the satisfaction of having your views put before the public, many times a cash payment is also given to freelance editorialists.

Editorials deal with very current (often fleeting) issues. They are brief, and they deal with contemporary topics and examples. They are not meant to be lasting items of literature.

Most editorials set out to do one of four things: (1) support a stance or action; (2) disagree with an issue; (3) laud something (or someone); or (4) educate the public about a matter. Your purpose in writing the editorial will be to woo the people into reading what you have to say, help them comprehend your views, and then convince them that your position is valid.

Good editorials will have a natural zest to their approaches to writing. The copy will challenge, awaken, entertain, inform, interpret, and/or guide the reader. The readers of editorials are looking for reflective thinking, additional data on a subject and a clear interpretation of the meaning and significance of the issue under consideration.

Basically, there are sixteen generic topics which editorials focus on and deal with. They are values, trends, culture, patriotism, education, rights, science, business, technology, politics, laws, people, history, economics, health, and art.

The format for the short editorial (used primarily) in newspapers is as follows:

> Title
> News Peg Noted
> Personal Opinion Stated
> Rationale Explained

Such editorials range from three to ten paragraphs. They usually use a standard news peg to note the event, such as "Last Tuesday, Mayor Jones announced. . . ." or "In a recent congressional session, a motion was made to. . . ." Having summarized the item of conversation, the writer then offers an opinion on the matter. The transition into this phase may begin, "The danger in this action is, . . ." or "Another side to this issue is, . . ." or something similar. Having stated an opinion, the writer then justifies it with quotes, statistics, or lessons from history or similar documentation.

Magazine editorials allow more space for reflection and analysis. They follow a longer format along these lines:

> Title
> Announcement of Topic
> Summation of General Opinions on the Subject
> Agreement with/Reaction to Those Opinions
> Justification of Writer's Views
> Close/Challenge to Readers

This second format allows for a more detailed overview of the subject, a more intensive case for or against the issue and greater support of the writer's claims.

Every person who begins to read any kind of newspaper or magazine article will proceed from one paragraph to the next wondering, "How does this relate to me?" The editorial writer answers that most basic question by saying, "This is *how, why,* and *when* this item of news relates to you. Furthermore, this is how I feel you should react to it."

And that's what makes a good editorial. At least, that's how *I feel* about it.

Science News

In 1980 I read a book called *The Jupiter Effect* in which two Cambridge University professors predicted that on March 10, 1982, massive tidal waves, earthquakes, and tornadoes were going to ravage the entire earth. I subsequently arranged to conduct in-depth interviews with two leading physics and astronomy professors at colleges in Indiana to get their reactions to this book.

The two physicists explained to me in great detail (and in heavy scientific terminology) why the theories in the book were inaccurate and illogical. I then wrote a lengthy feature for the *Indianapolis Star Magazine* called "Doubting the Jupiter Effect." It was written in layperson's language and presented in an easy-to-understand format.

My article appeared on Sunday, September 18, 1980. The next morning, to my great surprise, summaries of the article were carried nationwide by United Press International and Associated Press. Naturally, the wire stories gave credit to me for breaking the story. As a result, I was besieged with phone calls from a wide variety of publications asking if I had other scientific freelance articles for sale. I wound up with a dozen new assignments, ranging from an article on how the Bethlehem star was formed to a two-part series on how scientists measure fluoride levels in packaged foods.

My experience with the Jupiter-effect article proved to me that there is a large audience of readers who are interested in reading scientific news, if it can be written for them in layperson's language. It's an especially good market for freelancers.

There is big money in science and, so, there is big news in science. Each year research and development scientists receive more than $30 billion (3 percent of the GNP) to conduct their work. The United States has more than half-a-million full-time scientists and research engineers. More than $1.8 billion is given to two thousand colleges and universities annually by the government as support for research and development projects.

To the freelance writer, *science* includes everything scientists discover about nature, whether it's something about atoms, the stars, or the human body. It explores how things work and why. But science news also includes the way in which the information is used for practical purposes. It may be a new way to cure a disease or the discovery of a new fertilizer or the development of a more natural-looking hair dye.

Pure science deals in fundamentals, with the idea that understanding the queer, apparently trivial details about the universe will lead to a basic understanding of nature. *Applied science* aims at some amount of control over nature. Without technology, science is incomplete and inconclusive. Everything from medicine to commerce depends upon scientific fundamentals. That is why readers are drawn to such news.

Although science and medicine stories are interesting, they nevertheless must compete for their space in periodicals. As such, your science articles must be timely, interesting, and understandable. You should try to limit your article to no more than nine-hundred words and accompany it with drawings or photos whenever possible. Get to the point of the article immediately. Sentences should be kept short and all unusual or technical terms should be defined. Mathematical figures should be rounded off: Readers aren't interested in the fifteenth decimal precision of mathematics; they just want to know what the thing does. Usually, the more significant, definite, and widely applied any discovery is, the more concisely and clearly it can be stated.

Science reporters must be cautious about what they report. You should be skeptical of sense impressions. For example, experiments measuring the "brightness" of "really clean teeth" are too rough for more than general measurements. That makes it minimally interesting. Also, don't forget that every well-planned experiment is a question put to nature and that the experiment is biased by whatever the initial question is. You must judge, as a reporter, the validity of that question.

Keep in mind, too, what Einstein said: "Scientists make very poor philosophers." Scientists believe there is some logical order in even the most complex situations. As such, they will often tell you the makeup of something yet never recognize themselves what the grander implications of it are. You must discern that yourself and report it to your readers.

Similarly, scientists are usually poor at expressing themselves. Their analogies at times are clever sounding but often inaccurate. For example, a veterinarian once told me that "horses of a different color" all get along well together and, thus, people of different races should be able to do likewise. When I pointed out to the vet that horses don't even have the emotional or mental capacities for biases, prejudices, and

AIP Endorses Popularization of Science

The public relations division of the American Institute of Physics was asked in 1962 why freelance writers should make an effort to report science news to general readers. The AIP offered six justifications:

1. *Importance:* Science is part of the general cultural knowledge the same way art, literature, music, and drama are.
2. *Political:* Considerations for research funds at city, state and national levels make it necessary for voters to understand what projects are to be undertaken by whom and for what reasons, so that voters can voice opinions on these matters.
3. *Financial:* Since the ultimate financial support for science rests on laymen in public and private funding, science needs public exposure and notice.
4. *Bridging:* The media can help scientists show their sincere desires to bridge any gap of understanding between the arts and sciences.
5. *Suspicion:* If science wishes to dispell antiintellectual attitudes about its work, it must take direct responsibility to show what it is doing.
6. *Compatibility:* The aims of scientists and journalists are compatible in regard to seeking accuracy, and accuracy need not be sacrificed for interest.

---

preferences, he just shrugged his shoulders and said, "Well, you know what I was getting at." As a reporter, you must never mistake analogy for evidence.

Finally, remember that as science advances, the so-called "laws of science" must be revised. When I went to school in the 1960s, we were told that light could never bend, that Saturn had eight rings, and that mothers should lie flat on their backs for at least five days after giving birth. Today, light can be bent via fiber optics, space probes have revealed that Saturn has hundreds of rings, and new "mommies" are required to do daily walking after childbirth. So, understand that the laws of nature describe apparent behavior, they do not *cause* behavior; if nature does not follow the description, the laws must be revised.

The best way to report science news is to follow this format:

- A lead paragraph which grabs reader attention
- A follow-up paragraph announcing the actual news
- A paragraph quoting an expert on the subject
- Two or three paragraphs of background data about the topic
- Another paragraph of quotes from an expert or authority in the area
- One or two paragraphs forecasting the implications of this new scientific breakthrough
- A snappy closing paragraph which either summarizes the article or ends it with a reference where future information can be obtained

In marketing science articles, approach your local newspapers first, particularly if they have Sunday supplement magazines. Most small and medium-sized papers lack science writers on staff and will welcome freelance contributions. Later, you can expand your initially published article (nine-hundred words) into a longer feature for some of the national general-interest periodicals (in-flight magazines, tabloids, family magazines).

That's the nice thing about science: it impacts everyone, so it interests everyone.

Ethnic Publications

A writer is a person who is talented with words. That's what he or she is judged on, nothing more.

That's important to remember because far too often novice writers will close markets to themselves due to racial or ethnic biases. Reverse discrimination at its worst is when a writer says, "I'm white, therefore I cannot write for black, Hispanic, or Oriental publications" or "I'm Protestant, therefore I cannot write for Catholic or Jewish publications."

Using myself as an example, I can tell you that a great deal of the freelance writing money I earn each year comes from black-oriented magazines. If you check the Ayer's *Directory of Publications*, you will find more than two pages of listings of black-audience periodicals. Many of them—*Essence, ShopTalk, Black Finance, Ebony, Dawn, National Scene Magazine, Sepia, The Black Collegian*—pay hundreds of dollars for their freelance articles. To ignore such a vast and lucrative market is to put a ceiling on one's writing career.

A publication may have a certain ethnic or racial group as its target audience; as such, a certain portion of each of its editions will apply only to that readership. For example, articles profiling the leadership of the NAACP are not broad-based enough for publication in most general-interest magazines, but that same topic might warrant a cover story in a black-oriented publication.

So, a portion of any ethnic periodical will be for its prime audience only. However, the remainder of the pages in that periodical will contain material that will not have anything to do with race, creed, or heritage.

Here, for example, are titles of four features I have written for *Essence:* "How to Overcome Shyness," "Assertiveness Training for Your Child," "Managing the Time of Your Life," and "What Every Woman Should Know About Taxes." As you can see, these topics have no racial or ethnic application. The simple fact is, whether you are white, black, or any other color, you'll listen when somebody tells you how to save money on taxes or how to manage your time (or kids) better.

Therefore, begin there. Go back through your files of articles and ask yourself, "Is this manuscript something I could sell to an ethnic periodical if I updated it?" If so, send it off. Contact the various ethnic magazines and ask for their guidelines for writers. While you are waiting for them to arrive, spend time at the public library examining back issues of these magazines. Analyze their writing styles and observe their range of topics.

As you write future articles, ask yourself in what ways you can customize them to fit an ethnic publication. For example, if you are hired to do a general travel feature on a major metropolitan area, while you are at it you can find out which local politicians are strongly ethnic (profiles), which restaurants specialize in ethnic cuisines (recipes), which monuments in town honor ethnic heroes (historical features), and which theaters, museums, and concert halls feature ethnic cultural events (arts coverage).

Many times your ethnic features can focus on one topic, yet be covered from different news slants. For example, I once interviewed Don and Mary Giles, two young and successful black cosmetologists in Flint, Michigan. My first article on them was a business feature for *ShopTalk* which focused on the success of their beauty salon. My next feature was a separate profile of Mary Giles for *Executive Female* which explained how she ran three simultaneous careers as a hairstylist, accountant for General Motors, and a housewife. Later, I wrote about the publicity techniques developed by Don and Mary to promote their salon. That bit of writing appeared as part of my book *Become Famous, Then Rich*.

In profiling a person for an ethnic publication, concentrate on what will be of interest to that publication's audience. What is the profiled person's ethnic background? How does he exhibit pride in such a heritage? Does his career in any way relate to his ethnic roots? How has he been honored or recognized by clubs or organizations of an ethnic identity?

Keep in mind that ethnic pride is marketable. Not only that, ethnic cultures are fascinating to study. Writing about them not only puts cash in your pocket, it also broadens your social horizons.

Seasonal Articles

A few years ago an editor friend of mine phoned me on a hot July afternoon.

"Hello," I said.

"Merry Christmas," he responded.

I glanced at my wall calendar to confirm which one of us was crazy.

"It's ninety-three degrees outside, pal," I informed him.

"Maybe so," said the editor, "but I'm putting together the editorial content for my December issue today. I need your help. I want you to prepare a two-thousand word feature on ten inexpensive Christmas activities a single parent can plan for his or her family. I need it on my desk a week from now."

"A Christmas article? In July?" I protested.

"I'll pay you 25 cents per word," he added.

"Oh," I said, with a slight gulp. "Well, . . . in that case, . . . ho-ho-ho!"

That phone call has had echoes on a regular basis since then. The content is pretty much the same. Only the season or holiday changes. One editor may call in January with an assignment for a Father's Day feature needed for a June issue. Another editor may call in June wanting to know if I have ideas for a Thanksgiving article for the November issue.

The fact is, seasonal material must be submitted from six to eight months prior to publication, yet most freelancers wait until thirty to sixty days before a holiday before submitting articles about it. By then, it is much too late. So, editors often find it necessary to telephone stringers and to dole out assignments whenever they need seasonal articles.

Freelancers who write regularly for major magazines know that seasonal material is easy to sell if the holiday or seasonal article is unique and if it's submitted early enough. Most of these writers keep a copy of *Chase's Calendar of Annual Events* (Apple Tree Press, Box 1012, Flint, Michigan 48501) on a wall near their writing desk, but flipped six months forward. Thus, in August they are reminded that it is time to start submitting articles about Valentine's Day, Lincoln and Washington's birthdays, and winter skiing, sledding, and resort idea pieces.

Basically, here is what editors are looking for in holiday articles: things to bake, make, or send as gifts; party and celebration ideas; features on the holiday's origin, unique ways it is observed, and suggestions on how to make it more memorable or meaningful; tips on how to cut the cost of gifts, decorations, or travel; and profiles of people who are most directly involved in some aspect of the holiday (the grand marshal of

Ideas for Seasonal/Holiday Articles

Article Idea	*When to Submit*
"Rural Mail Delivery at Christmas"	July
"Antique Hunting for Christmas Ornaments"	July
"Choosing a Post-Christmas Diet"	July
"How the Indians Celebrate New Years"	August
"Tropical Vacations for Beating Winter Blahs"	August
"House Plants that Thrive in Winter"	August
"Coping with Winter Rheumatism"	August
"Nine Ways to Avoid Spring Pollen Allergies"	October
"Is Spring Fever Just a Myth?"	October
"Time to Plant Your Garden"	October
"Ten Harmless Jokes for April Fool's Day"	October
"Cold-cut Plates for Hot Summer Days"	January
"Decorating Your Summer Patio"	January
"Unique Locations for Summer Vacations"	January
"Summer Employment Tips for Teens"	February
"Is Summer School Right for Your Child?"	February
"Autumn Skydiving: A Fall in Fall"	March
"Painting Autumn Landscapes"	March
"Safety Tips for Pumpkin Carving"	April

the parade, a fireworks manufacturer, a turkey breeder, a department-store Santa).

Seasonal articles should focus on one theme, such as summer vacation ideas or spring housecleaning. They should be filled with suggestions, instructions, or book lists for additional references.

If you plan to query an editor with a seasonal idea, send the letter eight months prior to the season or holiday. If the query is rejected, you then will still have time to contact another editor.

Throughout the year keep a folder of "Holiday Article Ideas." Whenever you read of something interesting in a magazine or newspaper which you feel might make a good holiday feature, jot your idea onto a piece of paper and staple the article clipping to it. At the appropriate time, you can retrieve your idea and prepare your article. For example, in Fort Wayne, Indiana, there are two different Abraham Lincoln museums. Their public touring times were listed one day in a general "arts calendar" roster in the local newspaper. I clipped the tour time notices and attached a note to myself to write a feature about these museums for publication in February (the month of Lincoln's birthday).

You can start now to write about future holidays. As your payment checks begin to arrive, you'll come to see that *every* holiday can be "the season to be jolly."

List Articles

If you were to make a tour of your house right now to take a survey of the various articles you've clipped from publications and saved, you would discover that most are list articles.

In your medicine cabinet would be something like, "Five

Ways to Counteract Household Poisons." Held by a magnet against your refrigerator probably would be, "Eight New Tips on Dieting." Thumbtacked to the bulletin board near the phone would be, "Six Emergency Numbers You Should Know." Most of these articles would be yellowed with age and you would have long since forgotten what newspaper or magazine you took them from. You would remember that at the time, however, each had grabbed your attention.

List articles *do* grab people's attention. That's why editors like to buy them from freelancers and print them. List articles intrigue readers because they offer promises: they guarantee to provide a specific number of ideas, solutions, or facts for anyone who will read the articles.

Not only that, list articles are entertaining. Readers are amused by lists of whatever things are the best, worst, cheapest, most expensive, youngest, oldest, hardest, softest, kindest, rudest, happiest, saddest, blandest, or spiciest. Readers have an innate curiosity about what they might be missing out on in life. List articles respond to that curiosity.

List articles are extremely easy to write. They require no special knowledge on the author's part and only a minimum of research time (most of which can be handled over the telephone).

Often, the writer is his or her own expert source for a list article. That's how I frequently work. Once, after being bored during a three-hour layover in the Atlanta air terminal, I worked up a list of ten productive things business people could accomplish during layovers. I called the article, "Overcoming Terminal Problems." I sold it for forty dollars to *Roto,* then resold it for sixty dollars to *Market Builder,* then sold it for $125 to *Gulfshore Life,* and finally wound up using

A List of Potential "List Featues"
About Your Hometown

1. The Four Most Expensive Animals at City Zoo
2. Six Unidentifiable Items Found in an Antique Store
3. Our Library's Ten Most-Requested Classic Books
4. The Five Oldest Businesses on Main Street
5. The Ten Oldest Tombstones in the Village Graveyard
6. Four Doctors Share Their Funniest Experiences
7. Profiles of Three Husband-Wife Business Teams
8. Five Politicians Reveal Their New Year's Resolutions
9. Nine Ways to Reduce Local Taxes
10. The Eight Best Days to Visit Your Child's School
11. Four Pie Recipes from Retired Cooks
12. Three Reasons for Spending Your Vacation Here
13. Seven Ministers' Wives Discuss Child Rearing
14. Six Obscure Landmark Plaques Revealed Locally
15. The Three Most Dangerous Intersections in Town

it as part of Chapter 2 of my book *Staying Ahead of Time*. That's another thing about list articles: they have a wide range of audience appeal.

List articles are straightforward. Their three-part format is basic: a lead paragraph which explains the parameters of the list and verifies its usefulness; the list itself (presented numerically or with checks or other designations); and the close (which either summarizes the article or motivates/challenges the reader to make use of the list's suggestions or plans or informative data).

Many times ideas for list articles can come from your friends. Listen carefully to what people complain about and then try to discover a series of solutions to those aggravations.

If your minister mentions that it's hard to get people to arrive on time for church services, you can write a feature for a denominational magazine and call it, "Six Ways to Get 'Em to the Church on Time."

If your neighbor complains about employee theft at his business, you can write, "Ten Tips for Internal Theft Control" and sell it to a business periodical.

If your great-grandmother says she feels lonely, you can write, "Five Ways to Brighten a Senior Citizen's Day" for a general-interest, family, or religious periodical.

Keep in mind that lists are more functional than stylistic. As such, just present your material in a sequential order. Don't worry about transition sentences, foreshadowing or any literary devices. Just present the facts.

Nothing else is needed.

Weekend Supplements

Learning about the freelance writing opportunities among the weekend magazine supplements of newspapers is like listening to one of those "good news/bad news" jokes.

First, there is the good news. Currently, there are eight syndicated national Sunday magazines (*Parade, Family Weekly,* and so forth) and more than two-hundred locally-published weekend supplements. Approximately 75 percent of these periodicals use freelance material every week. Furthermore, upon publication, an article's rights are returned to the author in most cases; this makes multiple marketing possible. Most articles only need to be from a thousand to fifteen-hundred words long (although two-thousand word articles *are* permissible) and bonus payments are given for photos and/or illustrations.

But, there's also some bad news. Weekend supplements pay poorly: although the syndicated magazines pay up to a thousand dollars per article, most local publications pay from five to 250 dollars with fifty dollars being the norm. Even worse, payments are usually not made until two to six weeks *after* the article has appeared in print.

So, the bottom line is, if you are looking for an easy place to break into print without a lot of effort, the weekend supplements are open to you; but don't expect to get rich by writing for them.

From 1977–81 I sold more than a hundred features to weekend supplements. Some were blockbuster articles, such as the exclusive interview I landed with Walter and Charlotte Baldwin, the father- and mother-in-law of the Reverend Jim Jones of Guyana (which I sold to *The Cincinnati Enquirer Magazine* for 250 dollars, the Saturday "Michiana" magazine of the *South Bend Tribune* for a hundred dollars, and the Saturday "Roto" section of the *Fort Wayne News-Sentinel* for seventy dollars).

Most of the others, however, were general interest articles: a travel feature about Michigan's Calumet Theater for the "Detroit" magazine supplement of *The Detroit Free Press* (two-hundred dollars); a profile of a college professor for the "Weekender" section of *The Big Rapids Pioneer* (twenty-five dollars); and an interview with television actress Joyce De-Witt about her childhood in Indiana for the *Indianapolis Star Magazine* (sixty dollars).

Editors of weekend supplements purchase a wide variety of articles: investigative journalism, profiles of sports, political, and entertainment personalities, travel features, how-to features, and public forum pieces on education, business, or politics. The one criterion—for which there is no exception—is that the article must be of direct and obvious use to the readers within the publication's circulation area. For example, you might sell an article to *Parade* called, "Ten Inexpensive Colleges in America," but for *The Indianapolis Star Magazine* it would have to be either, "Ten Inexpensive Colleges in the Midwest" or, better yet, ". . . in Indiana."

Unlike national magazines which are published only a dozen times a year, weekend supplements are published from twenty-five to fifty-two times per year. Because of this, query letters are seldom used. Generally, the practice is to submit a completed manuscript with two to five (8″ x 10″) b/w photos and an S.A.S.E. Sometimes, after a writer has made six or eight sales to one editor, the writer can feel free to make telephone queries about current article ideas. A query letter is usually used only if the author's idea for an article will be costly to research and the writer wishes to see whether or not the supplement's editor will help pay for travel, meals, lodging, and other expenses. Both query letters and completed manuscripts should have the author's telephone number typed at the top.

One of the side benefits of writing regularly for the weekend supplements is that it makes a writer alert to all the big and small news items in his or her local area. One housewife I know writes just one feature per week for her area weekend supplements. That is the total extent of her freelance writing career. She explains, "Earning that extra fifty dollars per week gives me some spending money without having to work out of the home. It's just plain convenient."

Case Histories

ShopTalk magazine made its national debut in late 1983 as a magazine for black female cosmetologists. Although I was a white male who knew nothing about the beauty-shop business, I found myself listed in the masthead as a contributing editor before the third issue hit the stands. During 1984 the editor of *ShopTalk* paid me $3,850 as payments-upon-acceptance for eleven freelance articles. Why? Because I had one skill that made me extremely useful to *ShopTalk*. I was an expert at writing case histories.

Case histories are one-thousand-to-thirty-five-hundred word articles which are marketed to the more than seventeen-hundred trade, technical, and professional publications in this country. Case histories explain how a certain person or company solved a problem or learned to handle a specific task in a better way. Most often, case histories explain how to improve quality, save time, please clients, reduce costs, increase profits, or achieve productivity.

Editors of company house organs, corporate newsletters, and mass-marketed technical journals are in constant need of freelance material. Most trade and technical periodicals have limited budgets and a small staff. If an editor learns of a good story idea, he seldom can afford to pay for a staff writer and photographer to fly to and from that location for just one article. However, he usually is very willing to pay a freelancer who is already in that area to do the article for him. And, the most encouraging part is that the freelancer does not have to be an expert in the field he is writing about. He just needs to know which basic interview questions to ask and what article format to use.

I entered into the field of writing case histories somewhat accidentally in 1967. My father, an optician and ocularist, told me about one of his patients who had "lost" (lodged) a contact lens under her lower eyelid for a year. When the patient's eye was examined and the contact lens was removed, it was crusted with body chemicals. Since I was a college English major, my father asked me to write a brief summary of this case so that he could report it to one of the optical trade journals he subscribed to.

As a favor, I wrote the report, typed it, and sent it (with two photographs) to the editor of *The Dispensing Optician*. A month later—after I had long forgotten about the matter—a check for twenty-five dollars was sent to me. With it was a letter from the editor of *The Dispensing Optician* asking me to send more case histories to him. I was amazed. Back then, I didn't even realize that trade and technical magazines *paid* for articles.

In response to that follow-up letter, my father and I worked up two more case histories based on other patients. We submitted them. Both were purchased for thirty-five dollars each. I then started seriously poreing through my father's files and, together, from 1968–70, we found enough material to sell sixteen articles to *Optical Index, Optical Management, Contact Lens Reports,* and *The Michigan Optometrist.* Since then, I have written regularly for a variety of optical magazines, primarily *Insight.* In 1984 I was made a contributing editor of *Insight* and I received more than $2,750 that year for freelance articles on case histories and business articles in the optical field. The average payment for case histories between 1967 and 1984 had risen from thirty-five to 250 dollars.

My success in writing case histories for optical magazines led me to do similar writings for insurance magazines, music magazines, beauty shop magazines, and craft and needlework magazines. In each case it was just a matter of learning the terms and technical jargon of whatever the new business was and then interviewing people in that line of work. It can be done by anyone.

Nearly everyone you approach in any career field will be willing to talk to you. People and companies enjoy the free publicity they receive from profiles in trade periodicals. Your job is simply to tell them up front what you wish to discuss and which periodical you hope to sell your article to and then to assure your interviewee that you will allow him or her to "OK" your manuscript before you submit it. (This latter point ensures accuracy for your manuscript and peace of mind for the person you are reporting on. It's important to keep all doors open for future access.)

In writing a case history there is a basic five-point format:

Step 1: The Grabber. Each case history must have a lead that immediately "sells" the article to the reader. The lead should stress benefits, such as this lead which I used in an article for *ShopTalk:*

> Anne Wilson, owner of Anne's Wigwam in Evansville, Indiana, increased her beauty shop profits by 21 percent last year by setting up a corner display of wigs. This year she expects that market to increase by an additional 15 percent.

This sort of lead fascinates the reader who is in the same business. The reader thinks, *if I can learn how she increased her profits, maybe I can do the same thing.* To learn the facts, the reader will then have to finish reading the article. You've hooked him or her.

Step 2: Statistics. Each case history needs specific records. Important data to include are the names of the people involved and the business where they can be contacted. Also note the years the people have been in this profession or the years the company has been in business. Other items might include annual sales volume figures, the range of the company's products or services, the number of company plant sites and their locations, and the company's growth rate during the past five years.

It's necessary to report such "stats" because the reader will want to know by what authority the "experts" are speaking. A corporate lawyer with twenty-three years experience will be more impressive as a source person than will a new staff worker fresh out of law school. A company that has improved its production by 17 percent will be more impressive to report on than someone who merely has a theory about improving production.

Step 3: The Challenge. Having established your source's credentials, you then must state the problem the person or company faced. Usually, it's best to do this in dialogue, such as I did in a recent article in *Craft and Needlework Age:*

> "We were really up against a wall," explained Joan Lorell, owner/manager of The Crafty Fox. "We knew that if we used our limited capital resources to expand into ceramics, we might bankrupt the whole business if the new items didn't turn a profit in just four months. Nevertheless, it was our only option if we planned to compete against the new chain store in town."

You'll need to state the problem succinctly, describe its circumstances, outline both its risks and upside potential, and explain why it was necessary to face it at that particular time. Make sure the reader understands everything related to the matter so that prior to hearing how the problem was actually resolved, he can speculate as to how he would have handled it.

Step 4: The Conquest. After putting all the facts before the reader, it then is time to reveal how the challenge was met. In such reporting, you must explain both what *did* work right (so the reader can copy it) and what *didn't* work right (so the reader can avoid it). Be specific when you mention experiments, costs, time involved, and ways in which the final results met or surpassed estimates and expectations.

Step 5: Procedure. The case history should end with a concise summary of the newly adopted procedure. If new personnel were hired, give their titles and job descriptions. If a new "standard order of procedure" was adopted, break it down into stages and explain it step by step.

Support your explanations with five to eight b/w photos showing people performing the tasks at each stage. Besides shooting your own photos, request that you be given company photos of the people you will be writing about. If the company's own staff photographer took photographs of a development in progress (the construction phases of a new building, the remodeling of a shop, various training sessions held in-house for employees, and so forth), ask to review and borrow some of the prints. Also ask for copies of any company publications from recent months which may contain articles or news items about the case history you are researching.

In marketing your case histories, follow these procedures: (1) consult *Gebbes Directory* for listings of trade, technical, and professional publications; (2) ask people in your neighborhood, at your church, or at your social clubs to bring you sample copies of their trade journals and company house organs; and (3) visit a large metropolitan library and puruse its magazine room. Contact the magazines that you see use case histories and request a copy of their Guidelines for Writers.

When you query an editor of a trade or technical journal, there's nothing wrong with mentioning four or five case histories you would like to report on. If the editor rejects two and gives you the go-ahead for three, you'll always be ahead of the game.

I will admit to you that my sales to the dozens of trade and technical journals I've written for over the years have not gained me the same prestige as have my occasional by-lines in *Reader's Digest, Success,* and the *American Bar Association Journal.* Still, my case-history sales have kept me as busy as I have ever wanted to be and they've added seven-thousand dollars to my annual freelance writing income. Since prestige doesn't pay for groceries, I've no complaints about writing for the trade and technical markets.

Business Advertorials

A marriage of advertising and editorial commentary in the 1970s gave birth to a new form of writing known as the advertorial. During the 1980s it became an integral part of virtually every magazine and newspaper in the country. In fact, advertorials became so common, publishers finally had to start helping readers discern which features were straight news stories and which were paid promotional items; they did this by typesetting the sentence, "This is a paid advertisement" above or below the advertorial. No doubt you've seen this frequently in magazines.

The interesting thing about advertorials is that despite the fact that they carry a disclaimer statement, the majority of readers still read them as news features. The chief reason for this is because most advertorials are filled with facts and helpful information and they often feature photographs.

Freelance writers have established themselves as the middlemen in the advertorial preparation process. Sometimes a freelancer will approach five or six local businesses, offer to write advertorial features about them (at a rate of fifty dollars per hour), and then turn over ownership of the advertorials to the clients. The clients then can buy space for the advertorial to appear as often and in as many papers as the clients wish. In this way, the client gets an advertorial he has full ownership of and the freelancer gets 150 dollars per client for a "work made for hire" assignment.

Another avenue is for the freelancer to approach the editor of a weekly shopper tabloid or a daily hometown newspaper with an offer to create an advertorial rotation page. In this situation, the freelancer agrees to find ten local businesses that will buy two-by-two-inch ads for their businesses for ten consecutive weeks. The ten different business ads then appear together on the same page once each week; but, along with the ads, each week there also is a feature article about one of the ten businesses. At the end of ten weeks each business has been featured once and has also had ten ads appear for it.

Freelancers can get paid in one of two ways for working up an advertorial rotation page: (1) by straight payment, such as eighty-five dollars per feature, or (2) by commission on earnings, such as 20 percent of the total revenue the ten ads will generate for the newspaper during the ten-week period. When working for modest-paying weekly "shoppers," it's best to ask for a guaranteed price per advertorial. When working for a daily newspaper, the commission rate will usually be more lucrative.

One freelance writer who I know to have been successful at earning a living by writing advertorials says it's best to work with minimalls. She likes to find a small shopping plaza with about twelve or fifteen stores in it. She contacts the owners of the businesses with the idea of pooling their money (usually around five-hundred dollars each) to create an advertorial page in the local newspaper for three months.

"I stress the fact that they will benefit three ways," says the writer. "First, each business will be given one large feature article during the three months; second, each business will be given a dozen personal ads during that time; and third, the page will benefit everyone since each time a customer comes to the shopping plaza to visit one store, he or she will usually duck into another store, too. The main thing is to promote the whole plaza so that everyone can benefit."

Seeing the logic of this, at least twelve business owners usually agree to sponsor the advertorial page for three months. The freelancer then contacts the local newspaper's advertising department and arranges for the ads to be designed and printed. The newspaper collects six-thousand dollars from the merchants (five-hundred dollars times twelve merchants) and then pays 20 percent of this money (twelve-hundred dollars) to the freelancer. In exchange for the twelve-hundred dollars, the freelancer writes one advertorial for each of the businesses. She gives one copy to the merchant and one copy to the newspaper. If she can write one per day, she is able to complete the job in two weeks without having to work on Sundays. Her average earnings equal six-hundred dollars per week. Not bad for freelancing, eh?

Many times the merchants who took part in the advertorial page the first time will follow that up with participation in another ten-, twelve-, or fifteen-week commitment to another advertorial page. This makes the freelancer's work even easier.

Basically, the only difference between an advertorial and a straight business article is that the advertorial will never say anything negative about the business it is profiling. Also, unlike a news story, sometimes an advertorial will actually include a sales pitch, such as, "So, come on down between 10

AM and 7 PM and meet Dale and Margie Jennings and see their fine selection of handmade furnishings."

Here is a general outline of how to prepare an advertorial:

(A) *Spotlight on the Proprietors*. Explain why the business owners or managers are qualified to serve their clients and tell about their ties to the local community (trustee of the school board, member of the Chamber of Commerce).

(B) *Explanation of the Business*. Inform the readers of where the business is located, when it is open, how long it has been operating locally, how many employees it has, the products and brand names it carries, the range of services it offers and what sets it apart from its competitors.

(C) *Announcements of Special News*. Give special coverage to announcements of expansion plans, pending new services, scheduled grand openings or relocation plans.

(D) *Salespitch to the Customers*. Make the reader aware of all inducements to shop at this locale. Mention credit cards, senior citizen discounts, holiday sales, availability of parking, credit terms, service after the sale, and pick up or delivery services.

Modern business owners are keenly aware of their need to maintain a very visible profile in their local communities. They are impressed by what the advertorial can do for them. This opens a great many local writing opportunities for freelance writers. There's no reason why you cannot have your share of this market.

"As Told to" Features

Not everyone is qualified to work as a freelance writer. I suppose that's a good thing. Otherwise, you and I would have too much competition and we'd be spending a lot of time in unemployment lines.

But just because not all people are writers, that is not to say that all people lack something worthy to write about. Quite the opposite is true. Many people have had personal experiences, business experiences, cultural, social, and religious experiences that are the makings of fascinating articles or books. Their only problem—and it's a substantial one—is that they don't have the professional writing skills needed to record and market their experiences.

That's where we come in. There's nothing to prevent these people from telling us their stories and allowing us to write them. This is done all the time. Such books and articles carry "as told to" by-lines and are produced as a team effort.

I've done several "as told to" articles over the years. The first time it happened, I was approached by a child psychologist at a leading Midwestern university and asked to take his research and convert it into a general-interest article. Another time, a magazine editor gave me three cassette tapes in which a successful insurance agent explained his sales techniques; my job was to convert the taped talk into an article. Yet another time, I spent half an hour on the phone with a fashion designer who explained to me about his new fall line; using my notes of that conversation, I wrote an "as told to" feature.

Generally, there are four instances in which the "as told to" story is employed:

(1) when a recognized authority, such as a professor, physician, or scientist, needs assistance in explaining his or her knowledge in layperson's language;

(2) when a famous person, such as a politician, actor, or

musician, wants help in publicizing his or her career by writing an autobiography;

(3) when a wealthy or successful person wishes to explain the secrets of his or her success but does not have the time or writing skill to do a book; or

(4) when an unknown person goes through an incredible experience, such as giving birth to sextuplets, being awarded the Congressional Medal of Honor, or winning the Betty Crocker Bake-Off, and an editor assigns a professional writer to help that person tell his or her story to the world.

If you are interested in writing "as told to" articles, there are several ways to line up assignments. One way is by carefully reading your local newspapers and discovering people who are experts in certain areas and then contacting them with the idea of working together on a book or article. For example, if you happen to read a notice of a retirement party for an ex-conductor of a railroad, he could be a good source for travelogues, nostalgia pieces, adventure narratives, or historical documentaries.

You might also want to place small ads in professional journals:

> AVAILABLE: Freelance writer specializing in "as told to" articles for trade/technical/professional publications. References available. Rates negotiable. Contact John Q. Writer, Box 119, c/o this magazine.

You can also send letters to publishers, editors, and literary agents announcing your availability, stating your rates, and presenting your credentials. It won't take long for job offers to start coming your way.

You'll need an answer for the first time someone calls you up and says, "I want to write a book about our family tree.

How much will you charge to help me?" or "I have tape recorded fifteen of my best sermons and I was wondering what your rates would be to transcribe them into a book manuscript."

I usually judge my rate on the circumstances related to the assignment. If the person I'm working with stands to benefit greatly from the publication of the proposed article, I insist on keeping the royalty check for myself. For example, at colleges if professors don't get published, they don't get promoted (the "publish or perish syndrome"). So, if my article based on some professor's research lands him a better office, a new title and a two-thousand-dollar-per-year raise, the least he or she can do is let me keep the check from the magazine.

If I'm commissioned by an editor to help someone write his or her personal experience story, I estimate how long the assignment will take me and I bill the editor at an hourly rate.

If I approach someone, such as a doctor or busy industrialist, and ask them to interrupt their professional schedules in order to help me write a magazine article, I share both the by-line and the royalty check equally with them.

When writing the "as told to" feature, you must pretend that you are controlling the other person's hand and that he or she is actually doing the writing. At times it will be strange. If you are a woman freelance writer preparing a man's article, it will seem odd for you to write something in the first person such as, "I love to hug and kiss my wife and smell her sweet perfume." But remember, although you are the writer, *it's not your story*. It has only been told to you and you are repeating it as you heard it.

Your writing should be filled with facts and anecdotes. Be sure to double-check all facts—spelling of names, exact dates, numbers, towns, quotes. Do not trust the memory of your collaborator. Use old newspapers, an almanac, company archives, and other references to provide verified statistics and data for your article.

Probe your collaborator for his or her recollections, feelings, opinions, and ideas. Try to discover the humor, pathos, irony, and optimism of every story.

Keep your "as told to" narrative lively. Use short sentences. Go easy on adjectives and adverbs and rely more on strong verbs and nouns. Keep the element of human drama out front.

Prior to submitting the article for publication, have your source person read and approve the manuscript. Have him or her sign a release for the story. Keep the release on file.

Once the article appears in print, you will receive several calls from potential new source people. But don't be surprised if former co-by-liners call you again. Once people get by-line fever, they find it hard to shake.

Public-Relations Writing

From a cash standpoint, the most lucrative freelance writing I have done has been in the area of freelance public-relations writing.

I was once paid eleven-thousand dollars to write a training manual and business film screenplay for an insurance company that wanted to train its agents to relate better to prospects and clients. Another time, a Canadian firm paid me nine-hundred dollars to write and design a direct-mail promotional flier for an autumn sale it had planned. I've also written material for optical stores, private colleges, churches, and even a member of the Michigan House of Representatives.

Most small- and middle-sized businesses do not have enough money in their budgets to hire full-time advertising agencies or public-relations representatives to keep their names before the public. As such, they frequently hire freelance writers on a temporary basis (one week, one month, one project, or one sales season). A letter of introduction with a list of your hourly rates can be sent to businessmen in your town. As need arises, they can call you for an estimate or a consultation.

In my book *Become Famous, Then Rich,* I offered the following definitions of facets of promotion:

Topics for Press Releases

1. Meeting announcements; follow-up reports on meetings.
2. Coverage of fund-raising events.
3. Reprints of important speeches; reports on and highlights of speeches.
4. Announcements of program sponsorships; internships; scholarships.
5. News about business support for the arts.
6. Policy statements which affect the community.
7. Business anniversaries.
8. Company promotions of personnel; new job assignments or titles.
9. Assistance to a worthy charity or community group.
10. Announcements of newly hired personnel.
11. Earnings reports.
12. Dedications ceremonies.
13. Announcements of special honors, awards, trophies, plaques.
14. Summary of remodeling; notice of facilities being upgraded.

15. Announcement of land purchases or pending move by company.
16. Attendance at professional workshops, seminars, conventions, conferences.
17. In-service training and local professional development.
18. New concepts of routine businesses.
19. Future challenges facing a business or profession.
20. Results of a recently completed survey.
21. Solving a problem common to many people.
22. Something routine which is done in an unusual or innovative way at your office, store, or manufacturing plant.
23. A local event which ties in to an item of national interest.
24. Biographical profiles of employees.

---

(1) *Public relations* is the term used to describe the full scope of deliberate actions taken by a company or individual in an effort to influence public attitudes.

(2) *Publicity* is legitimate news coverage of events related to a person, product, business, or organization. It provides background, related data, and current information.

(3) *Advertising* is the action of planning a promotional strategy which will be carried out by buying time on television and radio, buying space on billboards and handout fliers, and placing ads in magazines, newspapers, and trade or professional journals.

As a freelancer, you may want to specialize in certain areas (writing slogans or jingles, taking press photos, writing newspaper ads) or you may wish to diversify your talents and be a sole practitioner capable of doing everything. Public-relations writers are called on to design posters, ghostwrite speeches, draft radio-TV-newspaper-magazine ads and press releases, prepare newsletters and policy statements, write articles and interviews for trade publications and company house organs, and write the promotional copy for pamphlets, leaflets and fliers. The more training you can get in these areas, the more valuable you will be to your clients.

When you meet with your client, try to discover answers to these questions:

(1) Does the client want a short-term publicity blitz (such as a Christmas season promotion) or does he/she want a long-range public-relations strategy?

(2) How much money is the client willing to invest in this effort?

(3) What mutual goals can the client and I establish for this campaign?

(4) What P.R. efforts has the client already tried and how successful were they?

Usually, the best way to help a new client is by issuing a series of press releases about the client and his/her business (see sidebar for topic ideas). When this proves successful, you can progress to designing paid ads and then arranging for public visibility through trade and professional journals.

In establishing your rates, simply add up the total amount of money you earned on your latest three freelance article sales (Example: $60+$325+$100=$485) and then add the number of hours it took you to write and submit the articles (2+8+6=16 hours) and then divide the cash earned by the hours involved ($485÷16=approx. $30/hr.). When a client then asks you to write press releases or advertising brochures, estimate the time you'll need and multiply that by your hourly rate (4 hours x $30=$120 bid). After that, you're in business.

Counterpoint Articles

In publishing, trying to jump on the popular topic bandwagon can often leave writers with sore backsides if their timing isn't perfect. The bandwagon frequently seems to move ahead too quickly.

Traditional wisdom holds that in order to be successful at marketing freelance writing, one must jump on the bandwagon—whatever people are excited about—and start writing about it. And sometimes that works, that is, if the bandwagon hangs around long enough for the writer to get something in print about it.

But my nontraditional experience has shown me that jumping off the bandwagon can often prove to be more successful. For one thing, there's virtually no competition when you're alone.

Frequently, when public opinion is leaning strongly one way, I purposely write a manuscript that supports the minority view. And, without fail (if my writing has been done well), I meet with amazing success.

In the late 1970s and early 1980s, the popular press was filled with articles and books which denounced workaholism. The workaholic was portrayed as a neurotic, masochistic, self-slavedriver who was chained to his job and who desperately needed psychiatric counseling. Everyone from respected physicians to pop psychologists on the radio was taking shots at the workaholic.

To me, these people were all wet. I had been a card-carrying workaholic since I was twelve and I knew it to be a great way of life. So, I said so in print.

In 1983 my book *Positive Workaholism* was released. It carried the subtitle, "Making the Most of Your Potential."

The book punched holes in the arguments of the so-called experts who had denounced workaholism as something negative. The book went on to teach people how to *become* workaholics by increasing their energy levels, using their time more effectively, and developing their mental strength to its maximum capacity.

The book was iconoclastic, singular in its view, and aggressively belligerent in its rebuttal of the then-popular negative view of workaholism. And the book was one other thing: incredibly successful.

It took off like a shot. In June 1983, *Success* magazine devoted an entire page to the book, giving it its highest praise. *Christian Business Life Digest* devoted two full pages to a review of the book and rated it four stars. United Press International did a wire story about my writing career and how I had conceived the "positive workaholic" theory.

Excerpts from the book were purchased by seventeen magazines. It became its publisher's top-selling book for 1983. In 1984 a company in Waco, Texas, purchased the audio rights to the book and made a successful cassette tape series out of it. I was in demand for appearances on radio and television talk shows from Fort Wayne to Seattle.

As it turned out, there were thousands of closet workaholics who related perfectly to what my book had said. They not only bought copies for themselves, they bought second and third copies to give to friends, colleagues, and spouses.

And the circumstance regarding that book was no freak one-time incident. About that same time, I wrote a long magazine article titled, "Why I Fought in Vietnam and Why I'd Do It Again." The article was based on my personal experience as a U.S. Army sergeant in South Vietnam in 1971. It argued that the United States had made a good decision to intervene

Phases of a Counterpoint Article's Lead

Why Mandatory Death Penalties Are Needed Nationally
By Fred Freelancer

People who have been against the death penalty as a deterrent to crime may soon need to reverse their opinions.

Opening Salvo

"Even though I hate to admit it," says liberal attorney Kim Davis of the Elkins, Davis, and McCormick law firm of Washington, "the fact is, states with the death penalty have substantially lower crime rates than those without it. Those sorts of results are causing more and more state legislatures to reconsider lifting the ban on state executions."

Credible Source

Recent statistics from the International Deputies Association show that hardened criminals who are pardoned from execution and subsequently released from prison return to a life of crime in 37 percent of the cases.

Additional Support Data

Law enforcement officials aren't impressed by statistical reports, however.

"Statistics? You want statistics?" says Federal Marshal Dave Ramsey of Crosscreek, New Mexico. "Well, here's one for you. Half the murderers released from prison go out and kill again. But 100 percent of the ones who go to the chair never commit another murder. Those are the only statistics a lawman can rely on."

Human Factor

in Southeast Asia and that there were many positive results which had come out of the Vietnam War. Obviously, this was not the popular opinion of the press media in America at that time.

The article was published in *The Baptist Bulletin* (May 1984) and the positive response it received even caught me off guard. Letters of praise and thanks came to me from the Pentagon, veterans' associations, editors, readers, clergymen, and writer friends of mine. Two Christian book publishers contacted me and asked for other samples of my works. One of those publishers later signed me to two major book contracts, one of which included a research expense budget which paid for a ten-day trip to the Orient for me in August, 1984. All that, simply because I was willing to verbalize the views of a silent, but unified, minority segment of society.

A recent best-seller by Terry Cole-Whittaker titled *How to Have More in a Have-Not World* shows that other writers have discovered the marketability of the odd-book-out theory.

Cole-Whittaker took a look at lines in the Bible such as, "The meek shall inherit the earth" and "The love of money is the root of all evil" and decided they shouldn't be taken literally. Her book proclaims that God actually wants people to be wealthy, powerful, and prestigious. I am at complete odds with this woman's theology, but the fact that her book sold more than ninety thousand copies does prove that you can get rich by writing about nontraditional views on things.

When you consider it, there has been an element of tradition bucking in many of the nonfiction best-sellers of this decade. The underlying message of *The One-Minute Manager* was that, no, you don't have to attend college for six years to earn an MBA in order to be an effective manager; all you really need to do is learn the three basic concepts in this book.

And, whereas I personally feel that that book was a sham, I can't deny its incredible success.

So, then, since it's obvious that swimming against the popular literary tide can be profitable, the next step is to learn how to do it.

Step One is to *determine the current popular opinions*. Scrutinize the newspapers and magazines that come into your house. Clip any articles that seem to present a slanted or biased approach to any topic. Start a folder. Review it frequently. Group collections of articles that seem to have the same theme.

Step Two is to *make a list of counterpoint views*. On a piece of paper, make two columns. On the left side, list the themes of the various article collections you have gathered from your folder. On the right side, list the opposite viewpoints.

Don't worry at this stage about whether or not you agree with the counterpoint view; just list them. For example, in the left column you may have an entry that reads, "Blacks, women, and the elderly are often discriminated against." Across from that, in the right column, you would write, "Young white males suffer from reverse discrimination."

To expand this list, you can check the best-seller lists of *The New York Times Review of Books* and *Publisher's Weekly* and make a list of all the books which focus on the same topic from the same viewpoint. You then can determine what the opposite opinion would be. For example, in 1978 when gold rose to 830 dollars an ounce, the best-seller lists were burdened with pro-gold books written by Harry Browne, Howard Ruff, Geoffry Abert, Adam Smith, and Douglas R. Casey. That same year, a friend of mine wrote a well-researched freelance article titled, "Why Gold Will Crash to $250 an Ounce by 1985." The article sold its first time out (to an investments magazine which paid four-hundred dollars for it).

Step Three is to *examine the list for the most promising topics*. After coming up with a list of ten or twelve counterpoint topics, you must focus on the best opportunities you will have for developing credible articles. You can determine this by answering four questions in regard to each topic:

• 1 Do I have a strong enough personal opinion about this topic to motivate me to present it with my best journalistic talents?

• 2 Can I find experts on this subject who will allow themselves to be quoted as endorsing an unpopular view?

• 3 Am I certain that no other author has already written an article or book which presents this counterpoint view?

• 4 Can I think of at least five freelance markets which might at least entertain the idea of publishing such an alternative opinion on this topic?

Finding one or two topics from your list which will meet the criteria of all four questions won't be easy. However, those topics which do survive the screening will have strong potential for marketing.

Step Four is to *query editors and prepare the submission*. Writing a concise and highly focused query letter will help you clarify and pinpoint your approach to the counterpoint topic. Mail the query as soon as it's ready, but keep a copy to use as your article-writing guide.

In preparing your article, use an offensive rather than defensive writing style. Your lead should be an opening salvo which immediately informs the reader that you mean to take issue with a popularly held view. This lead should be followed by a statement from a credible source so that the reader will be forced to at least give your idea the temporary benefit of the doubt. Additional data (statistics, case histories, references) to further support your claims are also needed early in the article so that the reader will know that you are not writing an editorial but are, in fact, presenting a well-researched article.

It's important to bring in a human factor, too. The reader will be wondering what impact this whole concept of yours can have on him or her. You must respond to that by giving a dramatic statement or an anecdote or a projection which the reader will be able to identify with. (See sidebar for a sample article lead.)

The balance of the article will have three objectives: (1) to summarize differing opinions and to respond to them; (2) to help the reader see the full scope of the topic; and (3) to present enough facts, quotes, and examples to win the reader over to the author's viewpoint. Of course, that will require adequate research on your part.

Whereas, editors are not open to ludicrous counterpoint topic articles, such as "Cancer Can Improve Your Health" or "Street Gangs Can Control the Population Boom," they nevertheless are open to sharing minority-held views with their readers. Their criteria for accepting such articles are strict: thorough research; credible sources; excellent writing.

Meet those requirements and you'll earn yourself an audience. Keep in mind that despite the fact that the current runs against it, a determined salmon can still make it upstream. So can you.

Freelancing Specialty Dictionaries

One of the most lucrative, yet virtually invisible, freelance markets is the writing of specialty dictionaries.

How lucrative is this market, you ask? Very, *very* lucrative.

Says writer Philip Morehead of Chicago, "My father was a lexicographer and journalist. He was the first man given a contract to revise and update *Roget's Thesaurus* for New American Library. I served as his assistant. When Dad died in 1964 I carried on the triennial revision work by myself. To date, the seven Morehead revisions of the *Thesaurus* have sold 15 million copies and I've earned a royalty on every sale."

At present, Philip Morehead is also earning royalties (and cash advances for triennial revision work) for his other books: the *Handy College Dictionary,* the revised *Hoyle's Rules of Games,* the *NAL Spanish-English Dictionary,* and the *Crossword Puzzle Dictionary,* all from New American Library.

"These books are timeless in that they do not come in and out of vogue the way novels do," says Morehead. "Students, businesspeople, and researchers are constantly in need of basic reference texts. As such, once you write a specialty dictionary, you can draw royalties from it for as long as you want to keep it updated."

John R. Ingrisano of Indianapolis is also a freelance lexicographer, but he did not inherit the job the way Philip Morehead did. Ingrisano had it thrown at him.

He recalls, "I was editing an insurance newsletter in 1977 for the R & R Newkirk Publishing Company. My boss called me in one day and assigned me to write a specialty dictionary. It was to contain correct spellings and standardized definitions of words related to the life and health insurance business. The topic was something I was familiar with, but the procedure for writing a dictionary was alien to me. I had to wing it."

Ingrisano developed a research procedure which enabled him to write *The Insurance Dictionary: Life and Health Edition.* After leaving the company and turning freelance in

1983, Ingrisano used the same procedure to write a dictionary of cinemagraphic and video terminology and a reference book for salespeople. His procedure is one any freelancer can duplicate.

"For the insurance dictionary, I started with the basics," says Ingrisano. "I first located and assembled all the insurance dictionaries which had already been published. Most were incredibly out of date due to changes in federal regulations, the advent of computerized claim-filing systems, and the development of such new insurance products as universal life and IRAs. I methodically went through the dictionaries and made a separate list of the words that were still being used, but I ignored their outdated definitions.

"I next wrote letters to more than fifty insurance companies in the United States and Canada and explained my project. I asked them to send me any glossaries, reference guides, or vocabulary lists they had prepared for their agents. I enclosed a copyright release form for them to sign so that I could adapt these lists to my needs.

"I then wrote to the Internal Revenue Service in Washington and the Small Business Administration in Texas and requested copies of all insurance-related pamphlets and brochures which they had produced for consumers. I also wrote to the companies which trained insurance agents and to the various insurance agent associations and asked for their terminology sheets."

The next step for Ingrisano was to create a master list of contemporary insurance terms based on all the data he had before him. Since 90 percent of the material he had gathered from various sources overlapped and repeated itself, it was easy (though tedious) to find a consensus of opinion regarding which words were standard and current.

Five Steps to Writing
a Specialty Dictionary

(1) Assimilate all previous references on the topic.

(2) Ask associations, companies, and government agencies to supply you with related glossaries, vocabulary lists, terminology sheets, and reference guides.

(3) Create a master list of terms; alphabetize it.

(4) Add new terms and update the definitions of old terms.

(5) Have the completed manuscript proofread by experts in the field.

Alphabetizing the words was a rote job, but then came the big task—going back to each entry, studying all the various definitions of that word (or phrase), and coming to an acceptable basic definition of that entry's meaning.

"The interpretation work was a real challenge," says Ingrisano. "Something like *misnomer* could be defined simply as 'a wrong name,' but words like *insurance* and phrases like *group contract* took half a page to define."

After a hundred days, the first draft of the book was finished. Ingrisano then gave copies of the manuscript to an experienced life-insurance agent, to three attorneys who specialized in insurance law, and to one editor of a leading insurance magazine. All five red-penciled any entries which were vague, incomplete, misleading, inaccurate, and syntactically confusing. (Philip Morehead also has experts proofread his manuscripts before submitting them to the publisher.)

"To my great delight, considering the vastness of the manuscript (510 typed pages), not many changes were needed," says Ingrisano. "I reviewed the editing suggestions, revised the manuscript accordingly, made a final draft, and turned it in."

The book is now into its fourth printing. Ingrisano has been hired twice, as a freelancer, to revise new editions. The book's success has led Ingrisano to other similar jobs.

Today, from his home office in Indianapolis, Ingrisano solicits freelance lexicography business by sending his resumé, hourly rates, and some writing samples to various specialty publishing houses, business associations, historical societies, and public service organizations. Those needing a specialty dictionary can then contact Ingrisano for a bid.

There are two ways lexicography freelancers can get paid. Philip Morehead submits a standard book proposal to a publisher and receives a cash advance upon closing a contract; later, he earns royalties based on the number of books sold. John Ingrisano charges twenty-five dollars per hour for research and writing. He earns from forty-five-hundred to eight thousand dollars for a completed dictionary manuscript; half the money is paid in advance and the balance is due upon completion of the project. Ingrisano signs over all rights to the book to the client. When revisions are later needed, he charges twenty-five dollars per hour and usually earns about sixteen-hundred dollars for a routine updating of material.

Both Ingrisano and Morehead wrote their first specialty dictionaries by putting individual words and their definitions on three-by-five-inch cards. After alphabetizing the cards, they typed the entries in manuscript format.

"Everything is now done by computers," says Morehead. "I subscribe to dozens of trade and technical magazines. As I read and discover new words, I add them to a computerized word list which I maintain constantly. When a book revision is needed, I take the old program which has been inputted with the entire manuscript and I simply add the new words at their proper alphabetical locations."

John Ingrisano observes, "When I first accepted the challenge to write a specialty dictionary, I figured it would be a tedious chore which would draw minimum readership and low by-line visibility. In truth, the investigative work proved interesting, the published book led me to several new assignments, and the revision work has provided a guaranteed freelance income base for me. What more could a working writer ask for, eh?"

Summary

As I noted at the start of this section, the fifteen areas I discussed here are the most popular, but not the only areas of specialized freelance writing. By working to master these fifteen areas, however, you will never lack for assignments, by-lines or royalties.

—Dennis E. Hensley

5

Writing for Religious, Denominational, and Inspirational Markets

Writing for the religious, denominational, and inspirational markets is no different, structurally, from writing for other specialty markets. However, its content is extremely defined and specialized for each specific audience of readers.

When writing for a denominational publication, for example, you must know the denominational interests and beliefs and write articles about subjects that appeal to the denomination's followers. In writing for inspirational magazines, your subjects may be more varied and somewhat general, but the article must be uplifting and inspiring to the readers. Don't overlook the fact that other magazines not labeled "inspirational," such as *Reader's Digest*, some women's magazines, and organizational publications, also use inspirational material.

Many writers believe they have to belong to a certain denomination to write for that denomination's publications. They do not. It need not be so, provided you have either a good familiarity with the particular denomination (Presbyterian, Methodist, whatever) or important knowledge in other fields that people belonging to that denomination would be interested in reading about. The best denominational writers have both familiarity and knowledge.

The denominational press (sometimes called the religious press) today offers something for everybody. There are magazines for conservatives and liberals, and for all stages in between. There are magazines for the well-educated, as well as for those of limited educations. There are magazines for those in full-time religious work: theologians, ministers, priests, nuns. Other magazines are for laypersons.

Religious markets use unpretentious writing which is bright and energetic. Articles are written to help readers discover something (or recognize something) about themselves.

Gertrude Stein once said, "If we knew everything beforehand, all would be dictation, not creation." Reading, then, is your best research tool for creating articles and stories for these specialized markets. Because writers are always advised to read as much as they possibly can in order to increase knowledge, they sometimes overlook the fact that through reading, they find ideas to write about, while at the same time studying other writing styles and editorial formats.

Successful writers get ideas from their daily newspapers. The religion sections in the newspapers—local, regional and national—list a smorgasbord of meetings being held in town and nationwide. Get on the mailing lists for these various denominational organizations and clubs. Also ask to be put on the mailing list of local churches, vocational schools, and libraries to receive notices of upcoming events. When you receive news of a meeting, look for the name of the speaker and think of the possibilities of obtaining interviews with ministers, priests, and other people in church news. Meetings mean ideas, articles, stories, and money for writers with initiative. Follow through with these contacts. Remember also that motivational and self-help lectures will provide a share of subjects and material for general inspirational articles.

Don't attempt to write for the religious press until you first spend some time getting familiar with the various types of magazines published for each religion or denomination you wish to write for. If your subject challenges the religious reader, the manuscript should go to a family magazine; however, it probably wouldn't be accepted by a devotional or inspirational magazine which is more concerned with developing the life of faith in the reader than in challenging that faith. Full-length articles, as well as short opinion pieces on social concerns, often find a place in religious magazines.

Writers sometimes believe denominational magazines are not interested in what the readers think, but rather only in the church's beliefs and teachings. But whereas it is true that some editors are less concerned about society as a whole than they are about the progress of the individual soul of the reader, it's also true that articles about marriage, family life, society, and even politics are always of interest, if written at a level a layperson can follow. In these articles you can discuss religious practices in a direct way.

Getting Inspired

To be an inspirational writer, read, study, observe, and take notes on how you feel when you see a beautiful sunset or look out your window and find the world blanketed in the first winter's snow. Make lists of the fine human qualities that appeal to you in other people, like compassion, the way people touch your hand when you're feeling lonely, the things people say and do to make your world more beautiful and a better place in which to live. All these things can be used to create inspirational writing that will bring hope and joy to others. What more could any writer ask for than this to share with readers?

Many people have an inspiring story to tell and the best

format for it is the profile or the as-told-to format. For example, you may know of a veterinarian who once a month sets up a free clinic to care for pets of the underprivileged people in his community, or perhaps a person who has overcome a handicap and is now helping others.

It's been proven time and again, by editors and readers alike, that people like to read about other people—what they're doing to improve themselves and the world around them, socially, politically, economically, and spiritually. Good writers for religious and inspirational magazines let the story speak for itself without sermonizing. If you can wrap up the events so that they teach without interjecting your own opinions and sermons, you'll succeed.

Articles and true stories you read in newspapers or in magazines can be rewritten as fiction, using the experiences of the people; or, they can be written as longer nonfiction articles once they are more fully developed. Personal experiences, too, provide ideas, as do the experiences others share with you.

If you're dry for ideas, see *The Encyclopedia of Associations* at your library. That directory lists thousands of associations and organizations whose members will be happy to give you interviews. You then will have many ideas to suggest to editors. Many religious organizations have their own publications and are willing to consider ideas or profiles of members for their publications.

Conversations with strangers anywhere—on airplanes, at the park, in a supermarket—will garner new topics and ideas. The old adage, "Never talk to strangers," was probably started by a nonwriter. After all, how does one grow and learn new things without talking to others? If you limit yourself to only the people you know, you will soon run out of ideas. Join groups and organizations and get involved with interesting people who are doing interesting things you can write about.

As an example, my three years work as a volunteer for The Arthritis Foundation garnered me seven feature articles about many interesting people I met through volunteering. Whereas I didn't really become an expert on arthritis, I did learn a lot about the disease—and about people. So, anytime you get an opportunity to become involved—in a walking club, your church youth group, the PTA, historical organizations, singles' clubs—take that opportunity to develop the new things you learn and new people you meet into salable articles and stories. Being involved is a requisite for being a successful writer.

Here's another way to get ideas. When guest speakers come to my church, I always attend for two reasons: to enjoy the message and to use the speaker's remarks as fodder for possible freelance articles. Sometimes I've written an inspirational article based on my pastor's Sunday sermon, rewritten in my own way, but using the theme and several quotes from my pastor. Anything worth a listen is worth mentally recording. Any specialized idea seems logical to develop for a specialty market. And remember that inspiration is meant to be passed along.

Study the table of contents page of the religious market magazines you'd like to write for. See what the issues focus on. Know who the readers are. Get ideas from one magazine's contents page to develop and write articles for similar markets. That's not stealing; you're only taking an idea and writing it in your own way. That's creative writing and marketing, and it's the way writers can make many sales.

Because it's impossible to read every magazine, you will need to find shortcuts to researching. There are more than four-hundred religious, denominational, and inspirational magazines. And there's more to their contents pages than just the list of articles and stories in the particular issue you're reading.

At a writer's workshop at Michigan State University, a *Reader's Digest* editor emphasized the importance of sharp focus and pinpointed theme when writing a query letter. "Too many writers sniff *all* the flowers in the garden without ever picking one," said editor Philip Osborne. Publishers and editors like to "trim the fat," get to the theme—one central idea—quickly. Or, as my grandmother used to say, "Cut the gingerbread."

Study closely the tone and style used in published articles. When you find a magazine you'd like to write for, ask yourself the following: Are paragraphs short, long, or a mixture of both? Is it a serious publication or does it occasionally offer humor in its columns? Are articles written in an anecdotal manner? Or is everything handled in swift summary fashion? Are statistics generally important to story development? How are titles and subheadings used? Does the editor break up a story into units? Are there sidebars, and if so, how are these used?

Editors sometimes have specific editorial styles that they insist upon maintaining. For example, Tom Walker, editor of *Continental* in-flight magazine, insists that manuscripts contain no one-sentence paragraphs. That information is stated in *Continental*'s guidelines. A simple matter, certainly, but important if you want to sell to that publication.

Study a few back issues of a publication and look for by-lines which appear again and again. Regular writers obviously know how to please the publication's editors and readers, so study the work of those writers to learn what makes their work click. Studying other writers' styles also helps you to improve your own.

It's a luxury for editors to explain, in a rejection note, why the style isn't right or doesn't work for their publications. Each editor has his or her own preferred style, but all editors understand and identify with all writing styles. *Writer's Digest,* for example, requires the mention of published examples in their how-to articles, just as some denominational magazines require writers to use examples of things happening in their churches throughout the country.

If an editor requests a "tighter style," or asks that you "tighten" the piece, it means you are to remove unnecessary adjectives, adverbs and sentences, any redundancies. "Cut it to XX-number of words" also means to shorten the manuscript by tightening the writing style. "Crisp" style is also used by editors to mean a "tight" style.

A "loose" style means the opposite, but not many editors ask for a loose style of writing, given limited editorial space. "Flesh it out" doesn't mean to just add flimsy words. It means you should insert more in-depth research or provide more solid examples.

If there is a religious magazine you wish to write for, a close study will help you write in the editorial style preferred by editors of that magazine. Editorial style, combined with your personal writing technique, should actually complement each other.

If you submit a manuscript and it is returned with a rejection note which reads: "Your manuscript needs more narrative," that means you need to insert more of yourself into the piece to lend authority or bring a more personal tone to the piece. The subject matter in many cases is probably suitable, but the editor is asking you to change the overall style—to include more narrative. If a rejection note reads, "Doesn't work for our crowd," it just doesn't work, whether it is because of the idea or the style of writing. However, every idea is worth consideration, so in most cases it is usually the writing style that is unsuitable whenever a manuscript is repeatedly rejected.

Some types of articles are popular and appear regularly in religious, denominational, and inspirational publications. Among them are the personality profile, lively reports of local church news, the think piece (what religious thinkers are saying about contemporary issues), national church news, personal experience articles, and coverage of unusual events.

Entering the Markets

Some areas in which freelancers are useful and needed are: writing newsletters (offer your writing and editorial skills to local churches); writing church reports and church histories; preparing press releases; promoting conferences. Get in on the ground floor. Become someone the church can depend on and you will gain experience, by-lines, and a reputation as a good writer.

Most interesting is the fact that denominational magazines often have finely honed editorial content appealing to a narrow readership. Some are popular intellectual magazines using articles about social and theological issues as they relate to the church in general and American religion in particular. However, the language is nontechnical, even though most readers are often college educated.

Family magazines, considered devotional magazines, are similar to general magazines, but they tend to stress some particular devotion or practice of a particular religious denomination. Mission magazines are completely devoted to the work of missionaries around the world. Broadening specialization even further, there are special magazines with articles about specific religious orders, students, or magazines covering specific liturgy.

What kinds of articles are preferred by most editors? One is the problem-solution article. Problems always exist. If you can identify a specific problem and want to write about it, here's how to go about it: Talk to three or more people in various careers, at different economic levels, in different geographic locations about the problem and record their suggested solutions. Write a survey lead which tells the reader what the problem is. Show its significance. Offer a solution (based on your interviews, your research, and your own experiences). Prove the merit of the solution. End with a challenge or a projection of some kind.

An advice article is similar, but much more personal in content. What you write about is how you, the writer, resolved the problem. If the problem is universal, it is best to talk to several people to give the solution more reliability and to call readers to action in solving their own similar problems.

Of the many kinds of articles, the narrative is perhaps the favorite and most widely used. It is a dramatic tale with emotional impact. The story is about something that has happened to you or to someone you know. Inspiring narratives are always in demand by editors. Another type of narrative is one that relates a personal experience or personal struggles with specific problems. It can be about health, personal relationships, or perhaps church involvement. However, of all narratives, those involving life-maturing experiences and spiritual discernment are the most meaningful and popular—and the easiest to write and sell. These articles appeal to all readers.

Guideposts specializes in such "spiritual take-away" narrative articles.

The ending of a personal-experience narrative should give direction and encouragement to readers who might be trying to cope with similar struggles and experiences. You really have to care in order to capture in writing the frustration, pain, remorse, or other emotions of the experience.

Another favorite kind of article is the list article, which takes only a few hours to research and write. To give you an idea of simplicity in list articles, consider these titles: "20 Ways to Pray," "10 Ways to Keep a Sick Child Entertained," "30 Reasons to Go to Church," "10 Ways to Make Someone Smile," "20 Ways to Make Holidays Happier." You can write list articles about any number of subjects: ways to achieve personal freedom, make your spouse feel needed, conquer work or family stress, enjoy your daily routine. List ten or twenty ways to do almost anything and chances are some editor will buy your manuscript to inspire or encourage readers.

Your own pet peeves can be a useful source of ideas for list articles. One writer was bothered by the fact that many churches today don't give their young people opportunities for creative expression, so he wrote an article that listed ten creative worship activities that could be used with church youth groups; he sold it to *The Youth Leader*. There are four kinds of list articles: the helpful hints list, the problem-solving list, the step-by-step list, and the "general-information" list. The most salable length for these articles is eight-hundred to fifteen-hundred words.

Quick profiles and short features are now replacing, for informational and entertainment value, the longer features which used to be published in periodicals. Profiles are interesting and fun to write, because the author gains information and knowledge by interviewing specialists and unique individuals. Profile research often leads to several other article ideas, too. If you haven't written profiles before, you might first practice by writing about yourself and what you find inspiring and later writing about others and their religious beliefs and activities.

Of all the specialty fields, religious and inspirational writers have the greatest number of subjects and types of writing from which to choose. Letters to the editor and book reviews are good break-in markets for beginners. Writing letters to the editor and commenting on a feature that has been published will be good experience for you and a way for you to introduce yourself, as a writer, to the editor.

If a magazine you'd like to write articles for publishes a book-review column, you might try writing two or three reviews of religious books. You can get the newly released books at the library or you can purchase a few. Get to know someone at your local bookstore. Tell that person you are a religious writer and ask him or her to let you know when new books are available.

As you read a new book, use a highlighter pen to mark the passages you think will be useful in recalling for your review. When you've finished reading the entire book, return to it and type in order all the highlighted passages and your comments about them. Then edit those pages to form a concise and flowing book review. Having a list of book reviews to present as a credits list is impressive, especially if you are widely read in a specialized field you later want to write for. This kind of reading and in-depth study of books for a specific denomination can only add to your store of knowledge. Quoting from books always enhances feature articles.

Fillers to the Brim

Writers find an open market for filler material in specialized publications. Fillers are usually fewer than five-hundred words, though some editors will use up to a thousand words. Fillers are epigrams, one or two sentences, either prose or verse; bright, witty, or inspiring thoughts tersely expressed; cleverly reworded proverbs; or plays on words. Short quotations also may be used as fillers. Fillers can be advice in one or two paragraphs, or hints that might be helpful to others.

Inspiring anecdotes are also used as fillers, and many Christian publications never seem to get enough of these. News releases can be written as fillers, too. News of your church activities sometimes sells to religious newspapers as fillers. Miscellaneous facts about anything or anyone can also be sold as fillers. Controversial or preachy fillers, however, have no place in the market.

Newsletters are intended to instruct, inform, and inspire church families, and should be written for all ages. Study past issues of the church's newsletters for style and format, presentation, length. Whether you are hired to produce a first newsletter or to take over the writing of an existing one, this kind of writing is extremely valuable. Gaining newsletter-writing experience—and especially if you gradually take over the complete project (writing as well as layout)—will one day provide you with enough experience to venture into writing corporate business newsletters, also. If you master the crisp and entertaining style of newsletter writing, you will be in demand in any number of other markets.

Because newsletters are limited in size, space is the first arbiter of editorial style. When writing for newsletters, follow these tips: quickly get into your subject (space doesn't allow introductory or "warming-up" paragraphs); use short sentences (one-word sentences are often used); use strong nouns and verbs, and limit adjectives and adverbs, which are crutches to weak nouns and verbs; use the active voice; develop a style of brevity; use *you,* because one-on-one is much more effective for newsletters.

Church brochures use freelance material. Brochures are created to attract visitors, instruct newcomers, and explain a church's purpose and strengths. Brochures are actually advertising tools and, as such, should be creative, well written, clear, and attractive. Collect and study brochures from many churches. Also study nonchurch-related brochures, such as those of business firms and nonprofit organizations. If you get an assignment to write a church's brochure, you will need to evaluate and write about that church's strengths. Does it have ample parking space? An unusual choir? Drama groups? Nursery care? Write about its people: pastor, organist, choir director, Sunday School teachers, deacons, elders. If the church has an interesting history, refer to it. Write down everything you believe might be a strong selling point, then edit later for focus after you've researched thoroughly. And always ask someone in authority to check the brochure copy before it is actually printed.

If you enjoy writing short stories or novels, you may also want to consider writing church plays. Drama for the church may involve biblical subjects, missionary work, character portrayals, or historical events. Learn proper manuscript formats by studying published plays, which can be obtained from Christian education leaders, libraries, bookstores, or play publishers. Many churches have drama groups and a church member who serves as director. Before submitting your play for publication, you might want to test it in a live performance; your church drama director can help in that area.

Curriculum writing is an appealing way to help people experience Jesus Christ. It demands as much creativity as other types of writing, contrary to what many believe. To be a curriculum writer you need not attend a seminary, Bible college, or secular college or even secure a communications degree. But you should keep abreast of current innovations by attending Christian education workshops to understand how long-range curricula are developed. Query denominational organizations and ask for curriculum charts and brochures; you need to know subjects, themes, and goals before you can create lesson plans for publishers. Editors of "take-home papers" also use articles, short stories, puzzles, and quizzes, which correlate with material used in the classroom. Think of this writing as writing to *teach*. If you can write how-to material, meet deadlines, and understand and interpret Scripture, and you don't mind teaching within the framework of another person's direction, you may enjoy curriculum writing. It's the most challenging, yet quickest way to communicate biblical information.

Many periodicals use devotional meditations. Writing devotional meditation involves sharing what you personally have experienced. If you wish to inspire comfort, challenge, or heal, you might try writing meditations. You have to care about people as individuals, be aware of their needs, and know where they hurt. You also have to be able to interpret events and happenings symbolically. A devotional filler may be presented as a narrative in which you tell the story of a personal experience or encounter that helped you understand some spiritual truth, and write it in such a way that readers will also understand and relate to that truth. A devotional might explain some insight you have gained about a particular Bible passage. Meditations have been written in book form for teachers, adult church members, single women, and others. The religious market is always in need for strong devotional material.

Also in demand today are articles written specifically for Christian singles. These articles are written for single adults of all ages. They use an informal style and are written with warmth and Christian dedication. Usually a personal touch is required, but there must be evidence of research, also. Editors of singles publications insist upon examples and case histories to maintain identification with readers. Subjects include single parenting, sharing, caring for others, Bible studies, relationships, hobbies, sports, recreation, and leisure-time activities appropriate for Christian singles. You don't have to be single to write for these publications.

Focus on Fiction

Religious, denominational, and inspirational magazines using fiction and short stories with an inspirational theme are other outlets for your creative efforts. However, the do-good-and-life-will-treat-you-graciously/do-bad-and-evil-will-befall-you slant doesn't work. Today's stories must focus on living in today's world, with all the pitfalls and joys. Salable stories do not consist of the old formula: crisis; prayer; problem solved. They must reflect true life-styles, believable characters, and happenings. You need to apply everyday experiences. When was the last time you read an inspirational short story that made you smile? These stories are, as editors will attest, difficult to come by, because they are challenging, though not impossible, to write.

You have to have something to say, and you must say it well. You have to discuss today's problems and fears, offer solutions and reassurances, and give solid examples of people who have coped with those problems and fears. The inspirational short stories you write must be carefully and thoroughly thought out before you can attempt to put them on paper.

Adult Christian novels today are consistently listed on lists of best-sellers, with the Christian romance being the most popular. The inspirational romance probably has been the fastest-growing phenomenon in the publishing industry in recent years. Interjected into the formula for romance novels is the need to include a message—something readers take away with them, to feel good about themselves and their own lives. The formula is not new, but the treatment is. Emphasis is on a romantic love relationship between the hero and heroine, with one requirement: that some aspect of Christian faith must be presented. Today's inspirational romances contain ten to twelve chapters, with approximately twenty pages in each chapter, or fifty- to sixty-thousand words per book. The author should lay the groundwork in the first few pages by introducing the characters quickly. Present the setting and conflict. Whatever keeps the characters apart during the novel—the conflict—should be resolved by the end of the book. In between is where all the work comes. That's where you write background material, provide the spiritual elements, and add physical descriptions. The spiritual element must be a natural outgrowth of the characters, shown through actions, words, and thoughts. Show that your characters have a belief in God and that sometimes that faith can be shaken. The marketing requirements for this kind of novel are the same as for any other novel.

Nonfiction Books

There are more than 140 religious and denominational publishing companies in the United States today. Some are well-established, familiar names—Zondervan, Word, Broadman, Tyndale, Augsburg, Moody. Others are newer companies, hybrids of secular houses, such as Epiphany Books (a division of Ballantine). Still others are publishing operations directly affiliated with a parent organization, such as Here's Life (owned by Campus Crusade for Christ), Navpress (owned by The Navigators) and Intervarsity Press (owned by InterVarsity Christian Fellowship).

Such a diversity of publishers also creates a diversity of manuscript needs. These publishers are currently releasing books which deal with a wide variety of topics, such as: archaeology; biography; Bible helps and studies; Christian education; church life; cooking; counseling; devotions; doctrinal issues and social issues; ethics; economics; evangelism; family life; health; history; marriage; missionary training; money; music; philosophy; psychology; science; sports; worship; and youth activities.

The focus of most religious-oriented publishers is on reaching the unchurched as well as the churched readers. As such, many nonfiction books released by religious houses have had tremendous success as "crossover" books. Marabel Morgan's book *The Total Woman* sold 600,000 copies in hardcover and 715,000 copies in mass-market paperback. Larry Christenson's *The Christian Family* sold 1,325,000 copies.

The success secret of these books was that they presented a Bible-based stance on a matter and explained it with an entertaining and captivating style of writing (which avoided religious jargon, churchology, and denominational catch phrases). These books filled a void, provided needed guidance, and inspired their readers.

Those nonfiction writers who have consistently produced popular and important books in the religious marketplace have accomplished this by focusing upon problems or concepts that readers relate to. They write about these topics from a perspective which is strongly based in the teachings of the Bible. Writers such as Catherine Marshall, Billy Graham, Corrie Ten Boom, Warren Wiersbe, Frances A. Schaeffer, Richard J. Foster, and Elton Trueblood have offered writing styles which have been bold in their directness and straightforward in their meaning. Readers have appreciated that.

To find topics for nonfiction books, many authors examine the articles which are given major space in the large circulation Christian magazines. Publishers often use this same tactic. For example, when Virginia Muir wrote an article for *Moody Monthly* on how to provide family home care for infirmed parents ("Three Generations Under One Roof"), she was offered contracts from three publishers who wanted her to develop her article into a complete book. She accepted one offer and wrote an excellent book. Magazine articles can sometimes whet the reader's appetite for additional information on a given topic. Books fulfill that function.

Book publishers can provide writers' guidelines to freelancers upon request. Most publishers want writers to submit an outline, chapter synopses, and two or three finished chapters, although some will ask to read an entire manuscript. Editors will want to know the author's credentials and qualifications for writing this book, who the book's target audience is, what the function of the book is (to inspire? to teach? to entertain?) and what similar books are already on the market. So, do your research in advance.

Poetical Words

Religious, denominational, and inspirational magazines use poetry in almost every issue, and many writers can turn their personal experiences into publishable poetry for any number of these publications. Writing religious poetry can be very rewarding, both spiritually and professionally.

Although John Engle would not consider himself a writer of religious poetry, I think of him when someone asks me to name my favorite inspirational writer. John Engle has a magical way of inspiring others through his poetry. One line from a poem of Engle's sums up life: "You have to live loving if you want to love living."

Poetry is a gracious form of expression. It's also an art in private communication, soul to self. Poetry writing can inspire you, but much more than that, it can be a lovely way for you to inspire others. Think often about your many personal experiences, your blessings, and even your struggles. Why not release those thoughts and feelings in the form of poetry? Writing then will work wondrous miracles for you and for your readers.

To clearly define religious poetry would be almost as impossible as giving one meaning to the word *inspiration*. To me, religious poetry and inspirational poetry have always been synonymous. The false belief that religious poetry is only about God or the beliefs of any given denomination keeps many writers from trying this wonderful form of writing. The door is open to anyone who can see the beauty of God in countless ways.

Poetry is the only writing form that is capable of taking on as many meanings as readers. The message is initially held in the mind of the poet, but is transformed into different messages held in the hearts of many readers. While a singular theme or idea is presented by the poet, many themes are generated in the readers' minds, making poetry almost a magical form of expression. In what other ways can you "say" something and have it "heard" so well?

The purpose of writing religious and inspirational poems can be twofold. First, for the writer/poet, a poem can serve as an emotional release of some great sadness or happiness in that poet's life. It might also be a way of "talking to God," of thinking things out on paper, to clear a struggling mind. But the purpose of religious poems takes a different view from the reader's mind. It might help the reader understand similar difficulties, share similar happiness, or work out individual struggles in an easy way. Obviously, the benefits of writing and reading this kind of poetry are limitless and much more rewarding than writing or reading general poetry.

There are as many kinds of religious poetry as there are experiences. Free verse, rhyme, expressive, experiential, contemporary, "see me." See me? That's the kind of poem beginners usually start out writing—and it's necessary for them to write the "see me" or "poor me" kind of poem. You have to go inside to find yourself and learn to express what's inside before you can accomplish the more mature "outside" poetry. To intimately know and express your own joy or sadness is the first step. Poems can be inspired and they can also be inspiring. We're all in this life together, and a poem is akin to reaching out and finding a hand to hold.

You can find poetry themes in many ways. I often find ideas by reading other poems. Like countless ideas, you can use the same theme another poet uses. You can then write your own poem: similar topic but different viewpoint. Poetry themes, too, lend themselves to longer article ideas. But they can serve as door-openers to many emotions and feelings that you have within you. You will be amazed at what freshness comes to you when you open those doors.

As you write one line at a time, ask yourself, is there another way . . . and another . . . and another, of expressing that one thought or experience? Sometimes fishing for other ways will provide fresh phrases of new and better lines. Don't be afraid to experiment with ideas and words. That's what makes fine poetry.

Once you learn to express yourself through writing poetry, you will want to market your poems. A good thing to remember is that you will find it easier to sell a poem that has a universal theme that most readers can relate to.

You will need no cover letter when you submit your poems. Most editors will read five poems at one submission. It's better to send several poems than to send just one—for that gives editors an opportunity to read more of your work and to have a selection from which to choose. Always enclose a self-addressed, stamped envelope for the editor's reply.

Gladys McKee Iker has written poetry all her life. She is regularly published in national women's magazines and other publications. I once asked Gladys how she developed ideas for her poems, and how she was able to write so proficiently and beautifully. Her answer was as simple and as inspiring as her poems: "Some days everything you touch is a poem." With that kind of attitude, imagine the inspiration Gladys finds in each day. She, like John Engle, has learned to love living and to write about the living she loves.

Learn to express the joy and beauty in your life and your poems, too, will be ready to share with readers who will find them enjoyable and inspirational. And as a poet, you will find your happiest writing experiences.

In a book title *Hostage to the Devil,* author Malachi Martin, a former Jesuit professor, says: "The mysterious truth is a bird doesn't fly because it has wings, it has wings because it flies." The truth, less mysterious, is: You're not a writer because you write; you write because you are a writer. And writing for the religious, denominational, and inspirational markets can be a great, satisfying reward in itself.

—Rose A. Adkins

Appendix A:

Frequently Asked Questions About Freelance Writing

Q. *Does it pay for a writer to be persistent?*
A. Yes. Without persistence, writers often fail. Persistence and discipline are the two most important qualities for writing success. Discipline is needed to get the writing accomplished and persistence for developing and marketing the manuscripts.

Q. *Does an author have to live in New York to be successful?*
A. No, nor does a screenwriter have to live in California. A writer can live anywhere and be successful. Editors are not impressed one way or another about the home base of a writer. They are only concerned about the content and quality of a writer's work. The only exceptions to this are the freelancers who are regional correspondents assigned to report on a specific region of the country or freelancers who need to be close to a project during major revisions.

Q. *Do I need a literary agent?*
A. Not at first, and perhaps never. An agent is useful only when you are selling almost every manuscript you write and are receiving so many assignments you cannot handle both the writing and the marketing of your work. When the business end of marketing your manuscripts is consuming much of

your time and becoming a chore that keeps you from writing, it is then wise to seek an agent. Agents are useful as negotiators when you become widely published and quite successful. If you have never worked with a book contract, it is advisable to obtain an agent or a lawyer to review the contract before you sign it.

Q. *Do editors prefer the work of older writers?*
A. No. In most cases, editors don't know the age of the writer—or the sex of the writer. And editors don't really care about age. If you have heard that editors prefer the work of older writers, it perhaps might refer to editors preferring the work of more experienced, polished, professional writers who have been in the business long enough to write manuscripts that are excellent and maturely written. Manuscript quality is what editors prefer, and it doesn't matter if the manuscript is written by a writer fifteen years old, fifty-one years old, or more than a hundred years old.

Q. *What are some of the problems editors have with writers and their submissions?*
A. Sloppiness is the main problem, such as single-spaced manuscripts, misspelled words, typographical errors. Factual sloppiness, which is the result of hasty or careless research, is a major problem, also. Duplication of recently published topics is another. Sometimes it's blatant laziness on the part of writers. Writers often ignore editorial policies and/or submission requirements. For example, if an editor prefers "no unsolicited manuscripts," writers are supposed to query first. Writers sometimes think they can disregard these required submission and editorial policies. This greatly annoys editors.

Q. *Why can't editors comment about why they reject my manuscripts?*
A. Editors are extremely busy, working under production schedules that are demanding and tight. Sometimes editors don't know exactly why they reject a manuscript. If they explain where they think a writer went wrong, they then take on the role of agent or critic. Editors are paid by their publishers to write and to edit, not to give advice about manuscripts. But what is unsuitable for one editor may be exactly what another editor is looking for; so, if you receive a rejection, select another suitable market and submit the manuscript elsewhere. The best place to meet editors and have them discuss your manuscripts is at a writers' conference.

Q. *Is it OK to offer the same idea to more than one magazine at a time?*
A. Yes, it's OK, but it's also risky. You may get more than one affirmative response. Then what? Multiple submissions are OK, but no question of professional ethics arises by selling to only one editor at a time. Multiple book proposals are a necessity today, however, and are encouraged. Freelance writing is, after all, a business, and should be conducted as such. Multiple submissions are a way some writers conduct that business. Literary agents use multiple submissions sometimes in order to conduct auctions for a manuscript.

Q. *What if I have not been published yet? Should I mention that in my query letter or my book proposal?*
A. Don't broadcast the fact that you are an unpublished writer. Instead, make your query letter burst with excitement and promise. If you have expertise (educational background or work experience) in the specific field about which you're

writing, it's useful to mention that in your query letter or book proposal.

Q. *I want to write, but I'm afraid I might fail. What advice do you have for me?*
A. Questions from beginning writers are more often laced with fear than with adventure. Stop worrying about failing and concentrate on your writing. Consider yourself a writer. Think of yourself as "a writer," and not just someone who is completing assignments. Write every day. Keep a journal. Feed your mind with the writing of others and study details and styles of other writers. Then push on and write your own voice on paper. Fear of failure has no place on the road to writing success, and in fact can block that road.

Q. *What are the chances of a first novel being published?*
A. There are a large number of first novels published every year, but one of the best ways to submit a first book is to get someone to formally or informally introduce you and your material to a publisher. Sometimes an editor of a magazine you've sold to repeatedly will introduce you to a publisher he knows. Or an author you meet at a writer's conference, if given the time to read your book manuscript, might be willing to introduce you and your work to his or her publisher. However, it is not impossible to sell a first novel without the help of someone providing an introduction. Make sure the manuscript is suitable in style and content to a publishing house, and send a strong proposal and outline. Carefully follow the publishers' submission requirements.

Q. *To what publishing house should I send my manuscript?*
A. No one can select a publisher for you. No one can suggest

an agent for you, either. Finding a publisher requires extensively studying available markets and matching your manuscript subject and style to what specific publishers prefer. Shotgunning your book proposal or manuscript to random publishers is futile. You must study the publisher's listings, read books they are currently publishing, and follow their editorial guidelines carefully.

A. *How many manuscripts are received each year by a magazine or a publisher?*
A. Several book publishers receive two thousand manuscripts or book proposals each year. Some magazines receive from one- to six-hundred manuscripts a week. *Newsweek*'s column "My Turn" receives nearly ten thousand submissions each year, of which only fifty are published. Because of the increase in competition, and high numbers of submissions, it has become even more important for freelance writers to submit high-quality queries and manuscripts which comply with specific editorial preferences.

Q. *What happens to my book manuscript when it arrives at a publishing house?*
A. If your manuscript is submitted after an initial query, at the request of an editor at that publishing house, it is directed to the editor who requested it. It is read first by that editor, then later by two more editors. If all editors agree the manuscript has worth, it is held for an editorial meeting which also involves people in the marketing and sales department. Patience is never a more important virtue than when you are waiting on word about a book manuscript, for it sometimes will take up to four months for the final decision to arrive. The editorial decisions and processes at publishing houses be-

come so involved and intricate, it is easy to understand why receiving final word about a book manuscript takes so long.

Q. *In writing for the trade magazines, is it possible to develop a style of writing or do editors prefer a specific editorial style of their own?*
A. Many editors welcome a fresh style of writing. Trade publications have for many years been unjustly considered dry reading. If you have sufficient knowledge about or can adequately research a topic you think might be of particular interest to readers of a trade publication, don't hesitate to write an article in your own style. Content is much more important to editors than style, and if the valuable and useful information can be presented in a fresh and inviting way, editors are usually pleased to discover such material. Their readers will find your individual style appealing as well.

Q. *For unsolicited manuscripts, is a cover letter necessary?*
A. No. A fluff cover letter is only burdensome for editors. Unless your manuscript is about a subject you are thoroughly involved in—for example, a manuscript about robotics in the medical field might carry more weight with the first reading if your cover letter states you are a physician or an engineer in the robotics field—cover letters announcing "I have enclosed a manuscript," or "I hope you enjoy reading my enclosed manuscript" are useless and time consuming. If your cover letter cannot enhance the manuscript, don't enclose one.

Q. *I want to get into a specialty field of writing, but I find it's difficult to conduct research about obscure and unusual subjects. Where and how can I find useful source people and source books on subjects that are more technical than general?*

A. There is a wealth of source books available on every possible subject. First, make a trip to your public library and study two reference books, *Encyclopedia of Associations* and *Subject Guide to Books in Print.* Check the key word index of *Encyclopedia of Associations.* Most associations have their own publications, just as most specialty fields have more than one trade magazine. Also check *Subject Guide to Books in Print,* which lists every book currently published in the United States. Listings are alphabetical by subject and field of interest. Then, of course, it's up to you to read everything you can find to increase your knowledge about a specific subject or trade field. Ideas for articles should be jotted down as you research these two reference books. Interviews can be set up with leaders of the various associations and organizations to further increase your knowledge and provide good quotes for articles.

Q. *If a specialty magazine uses poetry, but doesn't specify a preferred line length, is it OK to send the editor a 100-line poem?*
A. Usually poetry editors prefer poems four-to-sixteen lines, but if they don't give restrictions on length, it's OK to submit poetry of any lengths. Poetry editors are more concerned with poetry themes being suitable for their readers. It is best to obtain a few recent issues of a magazine and to read the poems published in them. You'll learn what type and length of poems an editor likes. You can submit up to five poems in one envelope, and, in fact, it is better to submit more than one poem, to give an editor a broader view of your poetry-writing skills.

Q. *How do you prepare a solid book proposal?*
A. A few basic elements make up a solid book-proposal

package: a cover letter explaining what the book is about and why you want to write it (or, in some cases, why you have written it or are still writing it); a sample of your writing (preferably a sample that will show the editor your writing style which will be the same style you'll use in your book); two or three completed chapters of the book (so the editor can see how you write and the treatment you plan to give the subject); an outline of the whole book (either a formal outline or a brief chapter-by-chapter description of what the book is about, again giving some idea of the style of writing). Your cover letter might also consist of a description of the audience for your book (who you think will buy the book and why) and a paragraph or two about any marketing suggestions you have for your book. Mention any special qualifications you have for writing the book.

Q. *If a magazine buys one of my articles, can I sell it to other magazines after it's published?*
A. It depends on what rights you sell. If you sell only first North American serial rights, one-time use, you can submit the article to other publications after it has been published by the first buyer. Many writers sell one article several times this way, submitting it to noncompeting magazines whose reading audiences do not overlap.

Q. *If I'm assigned an article by an editor who buys all rights to my manuscript, does that editor also buy all the research I did for the assignment?*
A. No. Only the manuscript you wrote for that particular editor belongs to that editor. You are free to use all the basic research to develop and write other articles, for other audiences, with varying slants. Writers who use their basic research only one time to write one manuscript for one editor

are losing the opportunity to make several more sales. It takes initiative and creativity, but research can be developed and rewritten many ways, thereby making it possible to earn much more money from basic research legwork.

Q. *I wrote what I thought was a good short story, only to have an editor reject the manuscript with a note stating that the story was "overwritten." What does that mean?*
A. Overwriting or overstating, sometimes called "purple prose," is a common writing problem for novice writers. It can be one of many things editors spot in a manuscript, such as redundancy, or using an excessive number of adjectives and adverbs, or writing too heavily with emotion. Also bad is contrived writing that seems unreal or forced, or writing that doesn't seem to fit smoothly into the story or theme. Some editors also refer to "talking down to readers" as a problem. This can be easily corrected, once a writer becomes aware of it. Keep in mind that overwritten stories can be edited, honed, and revised for eventual sale and publication. Almost all writing problems, when recognized, can be solved through rewriting and revising.

Q. *When conducting an interview recently, the physician I was interviewing made a statement that the interview was "not for attribution." What did he mean by that?*
A. He meant that the interview information can be used by you, but that he doesn't want you to quote him or attribute any of the information to him. Sometimes interviewees are willing to answer questions and provide useful information which can be used in your articles, but they don't want to be directly quoted or they don't want their names mentioned in the article. You can use this information by paraphrasing the person and attributing the material to "a prominent surgeon,"

for example, or "an authority in the field," without actually revealing the person's name. Of course, editors will usually prefer sources be named in the article, but depending on the strength of the information and value of that information in your article, and depending on how you use the material, it is possible to write and sell a strong article on a subject without revealing the names of your sources.

Q. *Many Christian publications mention in their editorial listings that they do not want "downbeat stories." What do they mean?*
A. Downbeat stories have unhappy endings. Unless your story can show something positive for readers, editors consider the downbeat story just a hard-luck tale. They prefer to offer their readers something positive that they can take away after reading the story—something that will offer a solution and/or solve a problem which they can relate to and learn from.

Q. *Can I use the name of a famous millionaire in an article I'm writing for a trade magazine?*
A. If your manuscript uses the name in a favorable way, yes. However, if you make negative allegations about the person, you should not use his or her name.

Q. *Many specialty publications list "think articles" among the kinds of articles they use. What is a "think article?"*
A. A think article is one in which a writer analyzes facts, trends, or events as the writer perceives them. The writer gathers authoritative opinions about a trend or subject, then draws conclusions that are intended to persuade readers one way or another. Similar to personal essays, think pieces also contain the opinions and ideas of others. Opinion-Editorial

(Op-Ed) pages in newspapers and in quality magazines use think pieces. Writers obtain the opinions of others through personal interviews, correspondence, and by reading books and periodicals. This gives depth to a writer's own personal opinions and feelings on a subject. Authorities in a specific field often *become authorities* because they write think articles that are accepted and published in trade magazines.

Q. *I have several good ideas for a specialty magazine. Should I send one idea at a time or do editors mind receiving a letter with multiple ideas and queries?*
A. Editors will often request writers to send a few ideas— just to see the originality and strength of ideas a writer has to offer. However, the most efficient way to send multiple queries is by typing one proposal—one idea—per separate page. You can submit several one-page proposals in one envelope. By querying this way, you allow the editor to respond to each idea individually and to return the one-page proposals that aren't of interest.

Q. *Do writers often become embarrassed when they realize they are unable to meet the deadline for an assignment? Do editors blacklist freelancers who fail to meet a deadline?*
A. Meeting a deadline is part of the professionalism associated with being a freelance writer. Some editors take the term *deadline* literally (i.e., "go past that *line* and you're *dead*"— no by-line, no check, no future work). In general practice, however, editors don't usually work on a production schedule so tight it allows no flexibility in circumstances concerning deadlines. If you agree to an assignment and to a deadline and later discover the research is taking longer than you had originally believed it would, it is best to contact the editor right away, explain the problem, and suggest another deadline that

might be more reasonable for you. Most editors will understand. If a writer repeatedly fails to meet deadlines or neglects to let editors know he or she won't be able to meet the deadlines, the writer will damage his or her writing career. In most cases, editors are more than willing to work with good writers to adjust deadlines. After all, that means bringing in a much better piece of work in the long run. Still, don't press your luck.

Q. *An editor replying to my query letter wrote that she likes submissions to be "quote rich." What does she mean?*
A. The phrase "quote rich" means articles should be heavy with quotations from people rather than general narrative written by the author. Read several recent issues of a magazine to see how the editor uses quotes in articles, and how quotes are actually presented in the text of published articles. Direct quotations are information presented in the exact words of your source—whether through interviews or passages from books and periodicals you used in researching the article. The direct quotes are enclosed in quotation marks in the manuscript. Indirect quotes can be paraphrased by writers, and are usually an abbreviated way to present information.

Q. *If I query an editor and receive a go-ahead for my article, should I then acknowledge that assignment by writing an agreement of terms to the editor?*
A. It isn't necessary to write an editor to let him or her know you agree with the terms of the assignment (for example, deadline, payment, and so forth). However, when you send the completed, assigned manuscript to that editor, you should include a cover letter with an opening sentence which reads: "As requested in your letter of assignment dated _____, I

am enclosing the manuscript, _____." Busy editors will sometimes assume a manuscript is unsolicited and treat it as such unless a reminder letter is enclosed with an assigned manuscript. A cover letter, therefore, will ensure that your manuscript is handled with expediency and not handled as a lesser-priority, unsolicited manuscript.

Q. *I have had several "Letters to the Editor" published in my local newspaper and in the general-interest magazines I subscribe to. Can these letters be used as clippings or tear sheets when I query editors with ideas for articles for various publications?*
A. Yes, they can serve as published credits. Include the names of the publications in which your letters appeared and the date they were published. Many beginning writers find letters an easy way to break into print, and a collection of intelligent, informative, and interesting letters will show editors that you do, indeed, have the ability to write well and to offer opinions in a concise and entertaining way. These letters will be most useful if you write pieces for Op-Ed pages in the larger-circulation newspapers and quality magazines.

Q. *I sent an essay to a trade magazine, but the editor rejected it with the comment that he only uses "objective writing." What is objective writing?*
A. Objective writing reveals little or nothing of the personality, thoughts, or feelings of the writer. It focuses on external things and events, and presents reality as it is—or as it appears to be—without interjecting any personal reflections, sentiments, biases, or emotions of the writer. Because the writer of an objective piece of work is not putting any of himself into the writing, it can be a difficult kind of writing to develop and

sell. There are, however, editors who prefer this type of writing over a more informal, personal style of writing. People who read publications which offer objective articles are searching for information that is presented quickly and directly. Readers do not expect to be entertained with this kind of reading.

Q. *Are there any ways to know whether an idea is a good one or not before I actually write an article?*
A. Although there is never a guarantee that an idea will eventually be sold to an editor, there are some things to think about when you discover something you'd like to write about. It's helpful to ask the following questions: Is the idea, or subject, worth writing about in a thousand or more words? Is it narrow enough so that almost everything important and interesting about it can be said in a few thousand words? Would it appeal to the focused interests of a specific magazine's readers? Is it a new idea or does it have something new to reveal to readers?

Q. *When I'm stuck for ideas, is there some way I can open my mind to allow new ideas to enter? How can I find more good ideas?*
A. Read two or three magazines you like and clip five or more articles you enjoyed reading. Could you have written those articles differently? Jot down the different ways you could have written about specific subjects. Read various newspapers for ideas, too. Clip articles that interest you. Jot down ways you could turn each subject into a magazine feature. During the day, jot down things that make you react emotionally. What irritates you? What pleases you? With the ups and downs of every day, always ask yourself why, and jot

down the why, because the answer might possibly be an article idea for you to develop. Make a list of everything you'd
like to know more about. Spend some time at the library
learning more about everything you listed. Ideas will come
from that list.

Appendix B:

Sample Literary Agent-Author Agreement

This AGREEMENT made this _____ day of _____, 19__, between _____, hereinafter referred to as the "AUTHOR", and ____(Name)____ LITERARY ASSOCI-ATES, hereinafter referred to as the "LITERARY AGENT."

Recitals

WHEREAS, AUTHOR is the writer and owner of a completed manuscript preliminarily entitled _____, hereinafter referred to as "MANUSCRIPT."

WHEREAS, AUTHOR desires to have the manuscript presented and placed with a publisher.

WHEREAS, LITERARY AGENT is engaged in the business of rendering its professional services to potential authors for the purpose of representing the interests of potential authors in manuscript placement and contract negotiations with potential publishers.

THEREFORE, the AUTHOR hereby engages the services of the LITERARY AGENT, and in consideration of the mutual promises herein contained, the parties agree as follows:

1. *Agency Term*. AUTHOR hereby engages LITERARY AGENT as his exclusive agent to the exclusion of all other persons including but not limited to AUTHOR, for a period of

_____ ( ) months, commencing with the date of this agreement, for the placement of MANUSCRIPT with a publisher. Upon placement of MANUSCRIPT, the term of this agreement shall cover the full publication life of the book.

2. *Placement activities.* LITERARY AGENT shall exert every reasonable effort to obtain the best possible offer for the MANUSCRIPT. LITERARY AGENT shall report to AUTHOR any offer that it obtains, and shall generally keep AUTHOR fully informed of its activities hereunder.

3. *Author's Acceptance of Publisher.* Any offer that LITERARY AGENT may succeed in obtaining shall be subject to AUTHOR's written acceptance, and shall have no binding effect on AUTHOR otherwise. AUTHOR shall be wholly free to accept or reject any offer. LITERARY AGENT's authority hereunder shall be limited to obtaining offers; LITERARY AGENT shall have no power and authority to close any agreement with publisher or make any binding commitment of any kind in AUTHOR's behalf, except as authorized by AUTHOR.

4. *Compensation of LITERARY AGENT.* If during the term of this agreement, LITERARY AGENT brings AUTHOR an offer that AUTHOR accepts in writing, LITERARY AGENT shall receive a commission for its services equal to ten percent (10%) on all AUTHOR's gross domestic royalties and AUTHOR's gross sales proceeds from the sale of subsidiary rights. LITERARY AGENT shall receive a commission for its services equal to twenty percent (20%) on all AUTHOR's gross receipts from the sale of foreign AUTHOR's rights.

5. *Royalty Collection.* All monies due AUTHOR and LITERARY AGENT shall be paid according to terms of publisher's contract. LITERARY AGENT shall promptly audit

royalty documents issued by the publisher for accuracy, report any discrepancies, and seek payment of any unpaid royalties.

6. *Photocopies of MANUSCRIPT*. MANUSCRIPT photocopy expense plus related out-of-pocket mailing and telephone costs advanced by LITERARY AGENT for AUTHOR shall be promptly reimbursed by AUTHOR to LITERARY AGENT upon submission of statements therefore.

7. *Sub-agent*. If another agent under the control of LITERARY AGENT is involved in any sale that LITERARY AGENT arranges, AUTHOR shall be liable only for the single commission specified in paragraph 4. LITERARY AGENT shall divide the commission with the other agent on such basis as he and LITERARY AGENT may agree; and LITERARY AGENT shall hold AUTHOR harmless from any claim he may make against AUTHOR for a commission.

8. *Independent Offers*. If during the period of this agreement AUTHOR receives an independent offer that AUTHOR desires to accept, regardless of whether or not LITERARY AGENT obtained a prior offer for AUTHOR, AUTHOR shall promptly turn said offer over to LITERARY AGENT for analysis and proceed upon the terms and conditions of this agreement. An "independent offer" shall mean an offer which has been received from a source not contemplated by LITERARY AGENT.

9. *Death of AUTHOR*. If AUTHOR dies prior to the expiration of this agreement, this agreement will be binding on AUTHOR's estate during the unexpired term of the agreement.

10. *Entire Agreement*. This agreement supersedes any and all other agreements, either oral or in writing, between the parties hereto with respect to the subject matter hereof, and no

other statement or promise relating to the subject matter of this agreement which is not contained herein shall be valid or binding.

11. *Assignment.* Neither this agreement nor any duties or obligations hereunder shall be assignable by the LITERARY AGENT without the prior written consent of the AUTHOR. In the event of an assignment by the LITERARY AGENT to which the AUTHOR has consented, the assignee or his legal representative shall agree in writing with the AUTHOR to personally assume, perform, and be bound by the covenants, obligations, and agreements contained herein.

12. *Successors and Assigns.* Subject to the provision regarding assignment, this agreement shall be binding on the heirs, executors, administrators, successors, and assigns of the respective parties.

13. *Attorney's Fees.* If any action at law or in equity is brought to enforce or interpret the provisions of this agreement, the prevailing party shall be entitled to reasonable attorney's fees in addition to any other relief to which he may be entitled.

14. *Governing Law.* The validity of this agreement and of any of its terms or provisions, as well as the rights and duties of the parties hereunder, shall be governed by the laws of the State of _____(State)____.

15. _____
_____
_____
_____

Executed at _____(City)_____, _____(State)_____, on the day and year first above written.

AUTHOR(s):

x _____ Address _____

x _____ City _____ State ___ Zip ___

Telephone ( ) _____

LITERARY AGENT:

_____ LITERARY ASSOCIATES

By _____

Appendix C:

Sample Collaboration Agreement

AGREEMENT made this _____ day of _____, 19____, between _____ (hereinafter referred to as "Author") and _____ (hereinafter referred to as "Coauthor").

FOR AND IN CONSIDERATION OF the mutual covenants and promises herein contained and of the mutual benefit to be derived hereunder, the parties agree as follows:

1. *Collaboration on Book.* The parties hereby undertake to collaborate in the writing of a certain book or literary work (hereinafter referred to as the "Book") dealing with _____ and provisionally entitled _____.

2. *Duties of Author.* Author shall:

(a) Supply to Coauthor all the facts and information necessary to enable Coauthor to write the book;

(b) Make available to Coauthor all of Author's diaries, memoranda, photographs, and like items pertaining to the hereinabove described subject matter of the Book;

(c) Make himself available to Coauthor for a minimum of _____ hours of total interview time within _____ weeks of the date of this Agreement, and at such other times and places agreeable to both Parties;

(d) Make tape and other recordings, if reasonably requested to do so by Coauthor, to clarify or simplify the materials furnished by Author; and

(e) Read and correct the manuscript of the Book prepared by Coauthor to ensure factual accuracy.

3. *Duties of Coauthor.* Coauthor shall:

(a) Do the actual writing of the Book; provided that Coauthor may, at his discretion and his own expense employ an associate collaborator to assist on transcribing of the tapes and/or in preparing the first draft of the Book.

(b) Adhere to the materials supplied to Coauthor by Author and not introduce any extraneous incidents or anecdotes without Author's approval;

(c) Proceed with reasonable diligence in writing the Book;

(d) Interview and consult with Author within _____ weeks from the date of this Agreement;

(e) Submit to Author the first draft of the manuscript when completed for Author's comments and suggestions;

(f) Make such changes in the draft as Author may reasonably request, provided that except when to do so would result in a misstatement of fact. Coauthor shall have the right to reject any such request if in his opinion such change would not be beneficial to the Book;

(g) Provided Author duly supplies him with all necessary material by _____, 19____, complete the manuscript ready for submission to a publisher within _____ months from the date of this Agreement; and

(h) Return to Author all the materials supplied by Author as soon as they have served their purpose, but in no event later than _____ months after delivery of the completed manuscript of the Book to the Publisher.

4. *Warranties by Author*. Author represents and warrants to Coauthor that:

(a) None of the material that he will turn over to Coauthor will contravene the copyright or proprietary right of any person or entity;

(b) None of the material will be libelous or violative of the right of privacy of any person or entity; and

(c) He has not heretofore made any contract or commitment that conflicts or may conflict with this Agreement, or impair Coauthor's rights hereunder.

5. *Copyright*. The copyright in the Book shall be obtained and held jointly in the names of both Parties hereto for the original and any renewal term of the copyright, and for any additional or new period of copyright which may hereafter be embodied in any copyright law throughout the world.

6. *Book By-Line*. When published, the Book shall bear the by-line of Author with some such legend as "with _____" or "as told to _____" on the cover and title page of the Book and whenever reasonably possible in the publisher's promotional material relating to the Book.

7. *Royalties*. All proceeds from publication of the Book and from the sale of subsidiary rights therein shall be divided between the Parties as follows:

(a) All receipts, royalties, and returns from the publication of the Book and from the disposition of any subsidiary rights therein shall be divided between the Parties as follows:

(1) Author shall receive _____ percentage thereof; and

(2) Coauthor shall receive _____ percentage thereof.

(b) All arrangements for publication and/or the sale of the subsidiary rights shall provide that each Party's share shall be paid directly to him.

(c) As used in this Agreement, subsidiary rights shall include without limitation the following: motion pictures (sight and picture), dramatic, radio broadcasting, television, book-club, digest, abridgement, condensation or extracts, photographs, anthology or quotations, reprint edition through another publisher, videocassettes or reproductions, first serial (pre-publication), second serial, syndication, magazine reprints, mechanical reproductions, records, reel and cassette tapes, use of title for commercial purposes and/or merchandising tie-ins, translation and/or foreign-language publication, and foreign publication rights other than above mentioned.

(d) If the Author purchases or acquires from publisher for resale or promotional uses any item(s) including without limitation any books, tapes, or records for which no royalty fees are paid by the publisher* thereof and for which Coauthor would have received royalty fees pursuant to sub-paragraph (a) of this paragraph, then Coauthor shall receive from Author a sum equal to the royalty fees which Coauthor would have so received. Said purchase or acquisition by the Author shall be deemed to be for the purpose of resale so that a sum equal to the royalty fees which Coauthor would have received shall be deducted from Author's share of the royalties prior to the issuance of any royalty checks. The amount of said sum(s) shall be based on actual orders placed by Author through the publisher's accounting department.

*(Explanation note at the end of this contract)

8. *Appointment of Literary Agent.* The Parties hereby agree:

(a) To appoint Coauthor as their sole and exclusive Literary Agent to arrange and negotiate for the publication of the Book and the sale or other disposition of any and all subsidiary rights therein, on such terms as Coauthor shall consider advantageous; provided that no contract or agreement for the publication of the Book or for the disposition of any subsidiary rights therein shall be valid unless approved by both Parties. As agent, Coauthor shall audit annual royalty statements for accuracy, report any discrepancies, seek payment of unpaid royalties, and otherwise protect Author's interest in the Book.

(b) If Coauthor shall perform the duties prescribed in sub-paragraph (a) of this paragraph, Coauthor's share of the royalties described in paragraph 7 above, shall be increased by five (5%) percent and Author's share of said royalties shall be decreased by five (5%) percent.

(c) If some person other than Coauthor is appointed as Literary Agent of the Parties, said person shall receive a commission of ten (10%) percent of the domestic royalties and twenty (20%) percent of all foreign royalties, half of said commission to be deducted from the royalties due each Party (Author and Coauthor).

(d) The person acting as Literary Agent of the Parties, if other than Coauthor, shall:

(1) Be named as a sole and exclusive literary agent of the Parties in the contract for publication of the Book and in all contracts involving the sale or other disposition of subsidiary rights therein;

(2) Audit annual royalty statements for accuracy, report any discrepancies and seek payment of unpaid royalties, and

(3) Promptly furnish the Parties with copies of any and all documents issued to literary agent by the publisher.

9. *Expenses*. In addition to any other sums which may be due hereunder, Author agrees to pay to Coauthor the sum of $_____ as a reimbursement for Coauthor's anticipated expenses to be incurred in connection with this Agreement. Said sum shall be payable as follows: _____

_____

_____

_____

(a) If publisher reimburses Coauthor for any or all of said expenses incurred by Coauthor in connection with this Agreement, the Coauthor will reimburse the Author for any amount the publisher contributes toward expenses, excluding advances on royalties due Coauthor.

10. *Negation of Partnership*. Nothing herein contained shall be construed to create a partnership between the Parties. Their relation shall be one of collaboration on a single work.

11. *Assignment*. Neither this Agreement nor any duties or obligations arising hereunder shall be assignable by either Party without the prior written consent of the other Party first obtained.

12. *Governing Law*. The validity of this Agreement, or of any of its terms or provisions, as well as the rights and duties of the Parties hereunder, shall be governed by the laws of the State of _____.

13. *Entire Agreement*. This Agreement constitutes the

complete understanding of the Parties hereto, superseding any and all previous Agreements, representations or promises, whether written or oral, between the Parties, concerning the subject matter hereof. No modification, alteration, or waiver of this Agreement or any of its terms or provisions shall be valid unless in writing and signed by both the Parties.

14. *Attorney's Fees*. The Parties hereby agree:

(a) Should it be necessary to engage the services of attorneys in connection with any dispute(s) concerning the interpretation or enforcement of this Agreement, or of any of its terms and/or provisions, whether or not legal proceedings are instituted, the prevailing Party shall be entitled to his reasonable attorneys' fees and costs in addition to any other relief to which he may be entitled.

(b) It is agreed, that in the event that legal proceedings are instituted in connection with this Agreement, that the place of performance of this Agreement shall be ____(City)____, ____(State)____, for the purposes of determining the proper place of trial.

15. *Successors and Assigns*. The covenants, promises, and conditions herein contained shall, subject to the provisions as to assignment, apply to and bind the heirs, successors, executors, administrators, and assigns of the Parties hereto.

16. *Article Headings and Defined Terms*. The article headings and titles to the paragraphs and/or articles of this Agreement are not a part of this Agreement and shall have no effect upon the construction for interpretation of any part hereof. Where the context so requires in this Agreement, the masculine form of any word(s) shall include the feminine and the neuter, and the singular form of any word(s) shall include the plural.

17. _____
_____
_____
_____
_____
_____

*Refers to the practice of publishers giving excessive whole-sale discounts to authors which permits cutting author and coauthor out of royalty fees (that is, 70 percent discount for purchase of three-thousand copies)

IN WITNESS WHEREOF, the undersigned Parties have executed this in the City of _____,
State of _____ on the day and year first above written.

AUTHOR: _____
Address: _____
COAUTHOR: _____
Address: _____

Appendix D

Freelance Writing Terminology

Advance. When an author signs a book contract with a publisher, the publisher usually pays the author an "advance" against future royalties. For example, if the publisher pays the author a one-thousand-dollar advance, that amount is later deducted from the author's royalties until it is worked off.

Author's Representative. An author's representative (or "literary agent," as he is more commonly called) is a person who represents an author in regard to publishing contract negotiations, paperback resales, overseas publications, and work-made-for-hire assignments. Lists of current literary agents may be obtained from The Writers' Guild of America, West 8955 Beverly Blvd., Los Angeles, Calif. 90048, and from The Society of Authors' Representatives, 101 Park Avenue, New York City, New York 10017. An agent's rates should be 10 percent on domestic sales and 20 percent on foreign sales.

Clippings/Tear Sheets. A sample of an author's writing which has been clipped from a periodical (clipping) or torn from a sheet of a newspaper (tear sheet) is often sent along with a query letter as a way of displaying a writer's credentials.

Coauthor. When two writers work together to write an article or book, they are considered joint creators, or "coauthors," of the finished piece of writing. Usually, both of their names appear in the by-line and they split the payment or royalties equally.

Credits Sheet. A credits sheet is a listing of all (for a novice writer) or select prestige markets (for an experienced writer) where the author has been published. Book publishers frequently wish to review a writer's credit sheet before risking a cash advance for a book project.

Expense Fees. If a nonfiction freelance writer is hired by a magazine to travel to a distant location in order to cover a story or conduct an interview, the freelancer should ask for "expense fees" to cover his or her air fare, gas and mileage, meals, lodging, and other costs incurred while in pursuit of the story.

Front/Back-of-the-Book Features. Most large, staff-written national magazines have regular short features or rotating columns in the front or back of each issue which are open to freelance writers.

Ghostwriter. Whenever a professional writer is hired to write a book which will bear another person's name as author, the real writer is called a ghostwriter. His or her name will not appear on the book. Ghostwriters are usually used when a well-known person wishes to write his or her autobiography, yet that person lacks the polished writing skills to make the book read well.

Hook. All articles and interviews need some sort of news peg or special slant which will attract a reader's attention. These leads are called *hooks* (or *angles*) because they figuratively snag the reader's interest.

In-house Operation. An in-house prepared magazine is one which is prepared by a hired staff and, therefore, uses no freelance material. An in-house publication is a magazine or tabloid which is prepared for workers of a particular company or corporation.

Journalese. Journalese is an umbrella term for all slang expressions or trade jargon associated with a newspaper.

Kill Fee. If an author is given an assignment and is promised to be paid a set fee upon satisfactory acceptance of his or her manuscript, he or she is also guaranteed a cancellation fee (or *kill fee*) in case the editor or publisher does not choose to use the completed manuscript. For example, if a writer is hired to write a freelance article for a payment of one-thousand dollars with a kill fee of 35 percent, the editor will have to pay the writer 350 dollars even if the editor chooses to reject or nor use the finished article.

Lead. The lead (or *lede*) comes from the typesetting term *leder lines,* meaning the opening sentences of a story or article. A lead must grab the attention of the reader and make him or her want to read the entire article.

Marketing. When an author seeks a publisher or periodical to purchase and print his or her manuscripts, the author is "marketing" his or her material.

Ms./Mss. The abbreviation *ms.* stands for manuscript, meaning the typed version of an article or book or short story as it is sent from the author to the editor or publisher. The abbreviation for manuscripts is *mss*.

Net to Author. In negotiating a book contract a publisher will usually offer a royalty arrangement which begins with 10 percent earnings for the author. It is up to the author or the literary agent to pin down in a contract if that means 10 percent of the cover price (retail) or of the price the book sells to the bookstore (wholesale) or of whatever the total earnings of the book are for the publisher (including volume discounts, remainders, and promotional copies). The ultimate actual cash that must be paid to the writer is the "net to author" agreement between the author and publisher.

Op-Ed. The sections of newspapers or magazines in which the "opinion" columns and "editorials" appear are known as the op-ed pages.

O.P. When a reader orders a book from a publisher and receives a notice that the book is O.P., it means the book is out of print; it is no longer being published.

Over the Transom. In past eras, editors used to work in office buildings which had an open frosted window (a transom) above their office entrance door. Since manuscripts in large envelopes could not fit through the small mail slot cut into the outer door, the postman would toss the manuscripts over the transom and let them fall into the office. Later, the term *over the transom* came to mean manuscripts which arrived unsolicited, since query letters obviously could fit through the door's mail slot.

On Account. If a publishing house has a best-selling author under contract to produce a book that may take two-to-five years to research and write, sometimes the publisher will loan money to that author "on account." This money may be paid back in a variety of ways: (1) from pending royalties from the author's previous books with that publisher; (2) from future royalties to be earned by the forthcoming book; or (3) by money earned from selling excerpts of the new book to magazines in advance of the book's official release. In the 1930s and 1940s editor Maxwell Perkins of Scribners frequently paid money "on account" to his most dependable authors, such as F. Scott Fitzgerald, Ernest Hemingway, and Erskine Caldwell. The practice is far less prevalent today.

Pen Name Pseudonym. When an author uses a name other

than his own for the by-line of his articles or books, the fictitious name is called a pen name or pseudonym. The pen name of Samuel L. Clemens was Mark Twain. The pen name of Evan Hunter was Ed McBain. The pen name of H. H. Munro was Saki.

Paragraph Rate. Rather than paying a by-the-word rate for freelance material, some magazines pay so much per paragraph, so much per column inch, or so much per page. Financially, this is usually to the author's disadvantage.

Payment upon Acceptance. With a "payment upon acceptance" agreement, an editor pays an author for a freelance article as soon as the editor accepts the article for publication. Most authors insist on this arrangement.

Payment upon Publication. With a "payment upon publication" agreement, the author receives no money for his or her article or short story until after it has been printed in the accepting magazine and distributed to the newsstands and subscribers. Thus, if an article is accepted in January and published in December, it will be a year or more before the author receives any payment or is able to attempt to remarket that manuscript to another publication.

Query Letter. A query (or questioning) letter is a one-page single-spaced letter sent to an editor outlining the idea an author has for a potential article. The query asks the editor if he or she would be interested in reading or buying such an article.

S.A.S.E. All query letters and manuscripts should be sent with a self-addressed, stamped envelope (S.A.S.E.) on the inside which the editor can use to reply to you at no expense to the magazine or book company you are contacting.

Sidebar. Any ancillary information which assists an article but is not put into the body of the article (such as a list of addresses or a sample quiz) can be set off in a box and printed along side the article.

Spec/Speculation. If an editor receives an interesting query letter from a writer he has never heard of, he may request that the author submit his or her manuscript *on spec*, meaning "on speculation." If the editor likes it, he or she will buy it; if the editor does not like it, the manuscript will be rejected and no kill fee will be paid. After an author has sold material to a publication and has thus established credibility, it is no longer proper for an editor to ask to see things "on spec." The editor should either reject the query idea or make an assignment for the article and establish a kill fee for it.

Think Piece. Essays and analytical articles which require above-normal concentration from the reader are termed "think pieces" by editors. Often, guest editorials fall into this category.

Unsolicited. If a writer sends a manuscript to an editor without first having solicited the editor's permission to submit the manuscript (via a query letter), that submission is known as an "unsolicited manuscript." Some periodicals that have a policy against accepting unsolicited material will send the submissions back unopened.

Appendix E
Writers' Colonies and Retreat Centers

John Cheever, Truman Capote, Irving Stone, Philip Roth, Katherine Anne Porter, Saul Bellow, Sylvia Plath. What do these authors have in common beyond their success and talent? All have, during their writing careers, visited a "writers' colony"—a creative retreat.

Truman Capote, for example, wrote *Other Voices, Other Rooms* in his quarters at the Yaddo retreat. And John Cheever wrote *Falconer* at a woodsy hideaway, which also gave him the opportunity to discuss world events with the caretaker.

Says author Joan Larkin: "Being at the Cummington Community of the Arts was an extraordinary experience, full of surprises. I knew I would enjoy being in the country for two months, but was unprepared for the powerful impact of this landscape on me. I was glad to be here long enough to begin trying to integrate it into my use of images in poems, but I know this is only a bare beginning." She adds, "I feel satisfied with the work and energized for the fall, surprised I did this much, as my general sense of my time here is of utter indolence."

"Having existed through school always feeling separate, misunderstood, unrecognized," explains writer David Mac-Bride, "being at The MacDowell Colony has given me a new outlook on my work—free of petty jealousies, paranoia, and other self-destructive tendencies." MacBride believes that being a part of a community "where artists respond to one another's unique vision of the world" was rewarding. "I will carry the benefits, memories, and warmth of MacDowell in my shirt pocket like a magic charm."

"Things I liked about Nethers Farm Retreat: being chased by seven goats, watching whole seasons change in minutes from blowing snow to sun, writing with a view outside my typewriter, looking up at night to more stars than I ever dreamed existed," says novelist Vickie Corey. "Things I didn't like: the way time whisked by double-time, seeing how citified I've become." And to poet Ron Morgan, Nethers was "like a prism."

Writers' colonies attract writers by the hundreds to work and write in an environment that feeds creativity. Some spend a week; others, a month; still others, three months or longer. Writers of all categories and at all levels have two common problems that, when verbalized, become complaints: *"I never have enough time to write"* and *"I have too many distractions."* Both problems can be solved by a stay at a colony. Because most colonies are nested in the byways of America, the beauty and serenity of their locations are in themselves lures. And, as poet Mark Baechtel described it after his stay at Nethers Farm Retreat: "After about an hour, the quiet inside matched the quiet outside."

Colonies also provide special opportunities for writers: individual attention to the writer's work, a listening and attentive ear, and encouragement for the writer's goals and dreams. Uninterrupted work on specific projects and the get-down-to-it intensive writing that writers often find impossible to do in their everyday environments can be easily accomplished at these retreats. Shared time with other writers is usually available if an author wishes that, too. Working alone during the day, and sharing an evening meal with other writers, and perhaps attending an evening lecture or reading or discussion period, afford a balanced and relaxing, yet rewarding, colony visit.

If you have attended a writers' conference, workshop, or seminar, you have experienced the excitement and enthusiasm writers find when they get together. The colonies, although quite different from conferences in that they are a quiet time for more solitary writing, also afford time for discussions with other writers as well as opportunities conducive to hard work and completion of projects at hand.

The fees for a stay at a writers colony vary greatly. The visit might be free. Some colonies offer you a stipend if you are accepted for residence. Others charge a fee that varies from minimal to quite extravagant; some colonies offer fellowships or financial assistance. Also, many colonies depend on "contributions" to keep going. Enclose SASE when you write to any of them for details about specific application requirements and activities. Most colonies make available brochures that detail fees, facilities, and length of stays.

Here are the addresses of some of the best known writers' retreat centers and writers' colonies:

William Flanagan Memorial
    Creative Persons Center
C/O Edward F. Albee
    Foundation
14 Harrison Street
New York City, New York
    10013

The Hambridge Center
Box 33
Rabun Gap, Georgia 30568

Millay Colony for the Arts
Steepletop
Austerlitz, New York 12017

Cummington Community
  for the Arts
Potash Hill Road
Cummington, Massachusetts
  01026

Curry Hill
Box 514
Bainbridge, Georgia 31717

Dorland Mountain Colony
Box 6
Temecula, California 92390

Fine Arts Work Center
24 Pearl Street
Provincetown,
  Massachusetts 02657

Nethers Farm Retreat
Box 41
Woodville, Virginia 22749

Yaddo Retreat Center
Box 395
Saratoga Springs, New York
  12866